WORD

Survey
of the
New Testament

WORD

Survey
of the
New Testament

Ronald A. Ward

WORD BOOKS
PUBLISHER
WACO, TEXAS

WORD SURVEY OF THE NEW TESTAMENT

Copyright © 1978 by Word Incorporated, Waco, Texas 76703.

ISBN 0-8499-0069-7
Library of Congress catalog card number: 77-92458
Printed in the United States of America

To My Wife

Contents

Introduction

SOME LITTLE TIME ago the publishers asked me to write a kind of New Testament survey. They were not interested in the usual questions of "introduction." Whether St. Paul wrote to the North or South Galatians did not exercise their curiosity. The date of the Fourth Gospel did not worry them and the Synoptic problem left them cold. As for form criticism and redaction criticism, the less said the better. They appeared to entertain the view that, far from being the exception, they represented the attitude of the bulk of the church. It is the content of the New Testament which is of chief importance.

The idea and the approach appealed to me. For a quarter of a century I have been involved in some way or other in matters of introduction and have been feeling more and more what a ripe scholar termed the "aridity" of much New Testament scholarship. And Charles Raven agreed with him. (I know this because I had the privilege of reading the scholar's learned manuscript and Canon Raven's appreciative comments.) Then I rediscovered Alan Richardson's remark that "we must put aside all modern critical notions when we try to understand how Jesus would have read the Old Testament."

Is it possible to do as our Lord did and still interpret the scriptures correctly? It struck me that God had given the Bible to the church, to be read and studied as our Lord read and studied the Old Testament. He received it as it stands.

9

Was he wrong? Has he misled us? Or ought we in obedience to learn from his attitude and teaching and receive the scripture more as a little child receives the Kingdom? The spiritual benefits hardly need to be explained.

It is possible to spend so much time tracking the movement of the stars that we fail to notice the sparkling brilliance of the heavens. We unweave the rainbow and forget its promise. We analyze the diet and avoid the meal; pore over the cookery book and never see a real loaf of bread. Yet some scholars, even in the critical camp, seem to endorse the pattern of Jesus when it comes to the life of the church: they support the work of the Bible societies.

The policy was settled long ago and is still followed. The scriptures are given to the peoples in their own tongue, without note or comment. But if they are studied uncritically, and if criticism is necessary for them to be understood, then the scriptures themselves may do a fearful lot of damage. If a man is given the Fourth Gospel, for example, without a warning to mind his step, without prior information that a writer worked on the tradition, put words more appropriate to the exalted Lord on to the lips of the historical Jesus, and reflected the church of his day rather than the days of his flesh, then a good many false impressions may be made.

What is the answer? If there is no danger, then the criticism is not vitally necessary to the life of the church. If the criticism is necessary, then either the clock should be put back a few centuries and the scriptures denied to the laity, or the Bible should not be published without careful and critical comment to guide the unwary who may believe what they read.

It may be doubted if either censorship or comment would be acceptable today in the publication and distribution of the scriptures. Can it be that God is calling us to devote ourselves to the text before we give too much weight to the criticism; or that the Bible itself contains the answers to the problems which it raises; or that we have been in danger of secularizing scholarship by an almost exclusive use of reason to the neglect of the Holy Spirit?

However these questions may be answered, I have tried to

concentrate on the text of the New Testament. In some academic books the authors tell us that they have used the English and have consulted the Greek. I ought to admit the reverse. I have used the Greek (because I am more familiar with it) and have consulted the English. The translations are frequently my own. The purpose has always been to bring out the meaning and to share it with the reader for his enjoyment.

Perhaps it ought to be added that this book has been written after a lifetime as a preacher. It would be agony to have to choose between scholarship and preaching. If it came to it, I could not give up the work of preaching the unsearchable riches of Christ. If we are sincere and right in our belief that God gives and owns the Word, then the mind of the preacher may have something to contribute to the mind of the scholar.

I hope that the man or woman in the pew who may read these chapters may taste the New Testament and find it good; and that there will be no delay in going on to eat and drink that which will satisfy all hunger and quench all thirst.

1.

The World
into Which the Gospel Came

IF ANY OF OUR FRIENDS suddenly began to speak of the Parisian Empire, we should probably raise our eyebrows and perhaps protest. "Surely you mean the French Empire? It is nations which have been imperial powers, not cities." Yet we take the Roman Empire in our stride. We are so used to it that we forget that Rome was a city.

In the period under our review it began as a city, and its history can be interpreted for some centuries as the story of expansion. At first it was bounded by what we should call "city limits." In time it was master of the lands which bordered the Mediterranean Sea. It still had its city limits; but its domain was a vast expanse: an inner irregular ellipse, the Mediterranean Sea itself; and all around the sea, in varying degrees of depth, the land.

The first area of conquest corresponds roughly to a large county. Latium was a coastal strip, a narrow plain rather to the south of Rome. Control here opened the way to supremacy in central Italy. Rome became a military power in Italy. Wars with the Samnites—and others—resulted in the subjugation of southern Italy. With Italy as a possession Rome was increasingly recognized as *the* Italian military power and one of the "Great Powers" of the Mediterranean— but at this stage merely one.

For just across the sea lay Carthage, a deadly political and commercial rival. At this time Carthage held most of North Africa, with a foothold in Spain, Sardinia and Corsica, and

Sicily. In the western Mediterranean she enjoyed a virtual monopoly of trade and command of the sea. Relations with Rome were "proper" and a clash seemed unlikely to come. But come it did. Both sides became entangled in a violent dispute being carried on in Sicily and they drifted into hostilities. The Romans gained their first limited objective and matters might have rested there. But encouraged by their initial success they pressed on to regular warfare. With enlarged appetite they set out to drive the Carthaginians right out of Sicily. It took them twenty years, in the course of which Rome became a naval power. Sicily became the first Roman province and Sardinia and Corsica were annexed within a few years.

Rome became a naval power; but her heart was not really in it. It was the army which was loved and honored. As the historian Theodor Mommsen tells us, the fleet "was always treated with the affection of a stepmother." Even naval battles took on something of the color of a land engagement. The Roman ships had gangways which they lowered and grappled to the decks of hostile ships, and over them poured —the soldiers.

Rome was still feeling her way, lacking the maturity, the experience and the methods of a great power. Yet she revealed amazing gifts of resolution, unanimity and sacrifice in the face of enormous setbacks. Carthage renewed the attack when Hannibal led his army over the Alps into northern Italy and was victorious in three battles, the first a skirmish, the others Roman disasters. The way to the south was now open. But Hannibal had no base, and central and southern Italy largely remained loyal to Rome. The Roman commander, Quintus Fabius, shadowed and harassed him but refused an engagement, thus earning the surname Cunctator, "the delayer." (Hence we speak today of "Fabian tactics" and "the Fabian Society.") Roman impatience forgot the wisdom of delay and their larger army was encircled and annihilated at the classic battle of Cannae.

In the end superior numbers and high morale turned the scale in favor of Rome. The war moved to Sicily, Spain and Africa. Carthage was unable to continue and ceased to be a

Great Power in the Mediterranean. Rome gained the conquered parts of Spain and from them formed two provinces, though unrest long continued; but she still had to contend with Carthage as a commercial power. She tolerated the position for half a century and then picked a quarrel. Carthage was besieged, captured and demolished. Her commercial empire had also gone. Her dominions became the Roman province of Africa. Rome was supreme in the West.

Meanwhile she had begun to build up her dominion in the East, where the Mediterranean had become almost a Greek lake. She was drawn into Greek affairs partly by the challenge of organized piracy in the Adriatic and even more so by an alliance after Cannae between Philip V of Macedon and Hannibal. Beginning with no deliberate policy of conquest she was led on by a series of wars to put an end to Greek political history; Macedonia was annexed as a province and its governor given authority to "interfere" with the city-states to the south; and the city of Corinth was razed to the ground.

Thus Rome expanded, and continued to expand, by conquest and even by bequest. At home there was a long struggle of sectional interests which developed into civil wars and the transformation of the Roman republic into the Roman Empire. The points at issue were economic, social and political. Economic crisis arose when vast estates owned by the wealthy meant the ruin of the "small man," and the extinction of peasant cultivators. Democratic aspiration encountered aristocratic antagonism. Two brothers, Tiberius and Gaius Gracchus, sought to bring alleviation by limiting the size of estates and redistributing land in small lots, and by a law to stabilize the price of wheat. Their work failed. It was only after revolt and war that full citizenship came to the Italians. Further cruelty and bloodshed attended Sulla's attempt to put the clock back and bolster up the Senate in the interests of the aristocracy. The ambitions of military leaders emerged, with private armies which remind us of the Chinese "warlords" of earlier days. Civil war ended with Julius Caesar becoming dictator. Prematurely he made himself a personal autocrat.

Caesar was undoubtedly master of the Roman Empire and stood alone. But even dictators can gain advantage from tact —and he was without it. He did not disguise his contempt for republican tradition, and signs and evidences of incipient kingship grew. Conspiracy inevitably followed: men with a chip on their shoulder and adventurers joined with sincere republicans, and even men in Caesar's favor, to plot his end; and their daggers accomplished it.

A struggle for power ensued, and the Battle of Actium in 31 B.C. brought to an end the republican government of Rome and ushered in the Roman Empire. Again we see one master, Gaius Octavius, the grandnephew of Julius Caesar. On his adoption by Caesar he was named C. Julius Caesar Octavianus. Within a few years of Actium he was given the title by which he is generally known, Augustus. It has no savor of royalty yet marks him off as greater than the ordinary citizen —"by divine permission" as it were.

An unofficial title is "Princeps," and the empire is frequently called the Principate. The somewhat colorless term goes well with the republican façade. For Octavian had the problem of combining republican sentiment with essential monarchical power. The old machinery of state had broken down; what was appropriate to the early city of Rome was inadequate to govern foreign possessions and fight external enemies. To change the high command every year or to assume that the successful civic ruler is automatically a military genius is not the way to run an empire. One man had to take the reins of government into his hands and that man had to be Octavian.

For consider: here was a man who had at last brought peace after years of unprecedented strife and massacre and terror, and was acclaimed accordingly by a people sick of it all; a man who alone controlled the entire military might of the Roman domain. If he resigned or shared his command there was no guarantee that "warlords" might not again arise to blackmail the civil rulers or renew the civil wars. For the sake of the public peace he alone must command the army. And with the army went everything else.

His own innate conservatism and taste, to say nothing of

the object lesson of Julius Caesar, gave him wisdom. He did not seek an absolute despotism and he sought to carry the people along with him. In consequence he preserved the ancient republican forms: he allowed others to hold offices and to administer them though he himself retained their powers and an overriding authority. He shared the government of the provinces with the Senate, taking care to keep for himself those which needed the presence of troops, such as frontier provinces. Foreign policy remained in the hands of the Princeps, the "first citizen," and to a great extent the administration of finance. He laid down the foundations of a professional civil service which long endured, aided no doubt by the wealth of Egypt which he had annexed as a province soon after Actium.

It is sometimes asked if Augustus deliberately deceived the Roman people in order to gain power for himself, or if he sought a genuine compromise between the jackboots of a despot and the chaos of republican government. Augustus was honest enough and not vulgarly ambitious. Thinking men no doubt realized the implications of his settlement, for an army is an eloquent argument; but they acquiesced. In that there are such beings as unthinking men, we can say that some may have been deceived. But they were not deliberately duped. And in any case, Augustus was indispensable: the Senate proved this by sincerely rejecting his offer of resignation. The premature Julius Caesar was outshone by the political maturity of his grandnephew.

Yet his brilliant success was not due to his own brilliant gifts—and his success was certainly brilliant. Augustus left his mark on the world. His work has stood the test of durability. He gave peace to the people and a constitution with a solid form of government, and both lasted for centuries rather than mere years. His general foreign policy was long regarded as a precedent. We look back upon an established tradition of government and law—and Roman law is still studied today. His civil service contained the germ of future development and in time it gave coherence to the empire itself, much as in modern times a nation has continued with excellent administration under an incompetent government.

But he was not the man to catch the eye as the obvious savior of the state. He was no genius. He had experience of military affairs and indeed of war, but was hardly a hero. He had not the charm which serves as a magnet, or the dynamic of leadership which rallies a flagging cause or leads the charge of thousands to the attack. He had little sense of "mission." He was no Hitlerite messiah.

How then did this unimpressive figure so impress? Historians, speaking as they do within their frame of reference, speak of luck, and we do not misunderstand their meaning. But it may well be within the providence of God that he "came to the kingdom for such a time as this." Caesar's old soldiers supported Caesar's heir. He profited by the mistakes of others, both friend and foe. He did not lack the advice of competent men in matters both military and civil. His long tenure of power, ensured by the military might of the empire which he alone controlled, gave him time and scope to test and amend. He was not self-deceived and claimed no "intuitions" which gave him instant revelations of what should be done. He could listen to advice and delegate to others, and could "feel his way forward." He could learn from his own mistakes and show patience and yet be resolute in implementing what he regarded as the right course.

Augustus died in A.D. 14, full of years, a "creaking gate" which had survived far longer than men would have been willing to prophesy. He was succeeded by Tiberius, who reigned from A.D. 14 to 37. The transition was an easy one: the first member of the Julio-Claudian dynasty, Tiberius was what today would be called a prince of the blood. He was the undoubted successor of Augustus, who had ensured his training for his new position. His position thus was strong. But he felt a certain weakness in spite of his qualifications. Augustus had designated a series of men as his successor but one by one they had been eliminated, mainly by death, leaving Tiberius as the only possibility. His feelings were like those of a bride who, though glad to be a bride, is well aware of the fact that three or four prior fiancées have died and by their death have opened the way for her. Again, the personal ascendancy of Augustus was the guarantee of the succession of Tiberius, but once he had become emperor he lived in the shadow of his great predecessor. Other things being equal, he would have understood the situation of a man who had been called to the pulpit and pastorate of a Spurgeon. He rightly occupies the pulpit; he is recognized as the pastor. But he knows, and if he does not know the people soon and constantly make it painfully plain, that no Spurgeon ever had a successor.

Trained in government and of proved ability, and possessing a strong sense of duty, he ought to have been at least a good "routine" emperor, not indeed inspiring his contemporaries but faithfully keeping the machinery of state in motion. To some extent he did not fail; the empire carried on. But he lacked self-confidence. Hesitancy made him reserved. He seemed to have no social warmth and in time became suspicious to the point of morbidity. Family feuds did not help. A policy of austerity rarely pleases people: unenthusiasm becomes criticism and ends in antagonism. Tiberius leaned heavily on one man, who intrigued against him in the interests of his own imperial ambitions until he was unmasked and dispatched as a traitor.

In weariness and disgust Tiberius had retired to the island of Capri. For ten years he reigned at long range, giving intermittent guidance by letter. The period is marred by the rise of informers and the sickening consequence of state trials or suicides of men whose only crime was political indiscretion or what was taken to be disrespect of the emperor. Far away in Palestine John the Baptist was beginning his ministry (Luke 3:1).

Tiberius died in A.D. 37, unregretted. His successor had not been chosen. But a son of a nephew of Tiberius, Caius Caesar, who had been kept at Capri, was imposed on the Senate by the Prefect of the Praetorian guard and accepted. He is generally known as Caligula, a pet name given to him by his father's soldiers when he was a small boy in camp. It is a diminutive of *caliga*, a soldier's boot which provided the pattern for the juvenile's footwear. Perhaps "bootee" is a fair equivalent.

It is an attractive picture: the small boy under the care of the commanding officer, his father, yet running about at large among the troops and perhaps even something of a mascot. It is not surprising that his accession was welcomed after the dark days of Tiberius. He began well, pleasing both the guardsmen and the populace. Some of his acts suggested a liberal approach. A certain apparent conscientiousness, combined with shrewdness and wit, confirmed men's hopes for a more enlightened reign.

It was not to be. He was devoid of training and of balance. He spent money wildly, in contrast to the parsimony of Tiberius. Led on by temper rather than statesmanship, he tolerated not even a breath of opposition and soon became a cruel autocrat with a policy of executions. Plot after plot was inevitably hatched against him until finally an irate guardsman cornered him and gave him a dose of his own medicine. The fire into which the people had fallen out of the frying-pan of Tiberius had lasted barely four years. Now it had been extinguished.

The throne was now vacant, but not for long. Caligula had an uncle, Claudius, who in terror had hidden himself in a remote place in the imperial palace. There he was found by some of the Guard. He was not of the prepossessing type, being timid, somewhat deformed and apparently an object of ridicule. But he was acclaimed for the sake of his brother, their earlier favorite. The guardsmen hauled him off to camp, forced the principate upon him, and then forced him upon the Senate. Claudius bound the soldiers to him by promising them a donative, thus setting a precedent for the purchase of the throne.

His reign (A.D. 41–54) had certain oddities. He had been a neglected child, brought up by servants and slighted for half a century. He had taken little part in public life and had retired to the world of books—and of low people. He was crammed with learning but short in judgment, a pedant like James I of England—"the most learned fool in Christendom" —and an author. He manifested a conscientiousness in his new position, some talent and a genuine concern. He could be fussy and yet shrewdly practical. At times he could fail to concentrate, or fall asleep in public.

Claudius was too weak-minded to resist the influence of his wives, the licentious Messalina and the masterful Agrippina, and the freedmen of his household. Emancipated slaves were not hitherto accustomed to offer advice in high affairs of state, but Claudius listened to them and they lined their pockets with the sale of offices. But the reign was not without its achievements, despite the graft. Claudius took a step towards humanitarianism, sought to ensure the wheat supply, undertook public works like aqueducts, opened the Roman citizenship to certain provincials and developed the civil service. Overseas a start was made on the conquest of Britain.

Imperial alarm, fostered from the distaff side, led to executions and a reign of terror for prominent men in the last few years. Claudius was inveigled by his wife Agrippina in plans for the succession when he died suddenly—perhaps poisoned by her. She had already made a deal with the new Praetorian prefect, and now he kept to his part of the bargain. Agrippina had a son by a previous marriage whom Claudius with some hesitation had adopted. The prefect introduced him to his guardsmen as the new emperor who had a bounty for them in his pocket. An "instant" principate was obtainable for cash.

Nero (A.D. 54–68) was still in his teens when he thus emerged into the imperial blaze: untrained and unfit to rule. His mother had hoped and planned to be the power behind the throne, but she was resisted by the prefect and her son's tutor, the celebrated Seneca. She overplayed her hand, and within a few months Nero sided with his two ministers and advisers. Agrippina lay low for three years and then resumed the conflict by interfering with Nero's matrimonial affairs. He rid himself of the nuisance by contriving her murder. It was an omen of things to come.

Even so the first few years of his reign were years of good government, thanks to the care and efficiency of Seneca and Burrus, the prefect of the guards. Nero's eccentricities were at first limited to a relatively small circle and not too widely known. But a turning point came with what we should call a change of ministry: Burrus died and Seneca retired, and

Nero fell under the evil influence of a new Praetorian prefect.

The Roman *gravitas,* a grave dignity which was the old Roman ideal, was abandoned—if ever it had been manifested. Frivolity and the pursuit of amusement became profligacy open and unashamed. Appearance on the public stage and a theatrical tour of Greece revealed the egocentric showman. Administration was neglected; government yielded to misgovernment; expenditure was unrestrained. The finances were disorganized to the point of bankruptcy. Nero began the process of depreciating the coinage which contributed eventually to chaos and collapse three centuries later.

Overseas the lot of provincials was being improved, a reason for their content as they did not at first realize what was going on in Rome. There the emperor stood revealed as another Caligula, irresponsible and autocratic. Decency was scandalized and wealth confiscated. Nero became the object of hatred and contempt. Needing scapegoats to clear himself of the charge of setting fire to the capital—of which he was innocent—he "framed" the Christians.

The pay of the troops fell into arrears. The nonappearance of their money led to the departure of their loyalty. A revolt broke out in Gaul, and "the year of the four emperors" saw the proclamation of successive emperors by troops in different parts of the empire—Spain, Rome, Germany, and by the army of the East and of the Danube. The wheel had come full circle. Nero had once more let loose a flood of professional informers for men's ruin. Now the professional soldiers turned on him. Nero was deserted and condemned; he fled and committed suicide.

Thus Rome expanded. Still a city, she dominated the known world, carefully but increasingly extending her citizenship but still ruling. This was the world into which the gospel came. Our Lord was born in the time of Augustus (Luke 2:1) and fulfilled his ministry in the reign of Tiberius. By the time of Claudius the church was in her stride in the spreading of the good news of the gospel (Acts 18:2; cf. 11:28). In A.D. 66 the Jewish rebellion broke out and the situation was well handled by Vespasian. He abandoned his work in Palestine on the death of Nero and returned to the

West to become the last and most successful of "the four emperors" (A.D. 69–79). T. Flavius Vespasianus thus was the founder of the Flavian dynasty. His command in Palestine was committed to his son Titus, who besieged Jerusalem for six months and finally reduced it. The Temple was destroyed and not rebuilt.

The destruction of the Temple was the outward and visible sign, in the divine mercy delayed for a generation, of the final apostasy of the Jews. When they should have been faithful to their one King, God himself (Judges 8:23; 1 Sam. 8:7; 10:19; 12:12), they cried out, "We have no king but Caesar" (John 19:15). When their own authentic King visited them in person to gather them under his sheltering wing in peace (cf. Matt. 23:37; Luke 19:41–44), they "would not." They did not recognize their opportunity.

The destruction of the Temple was an outward and visible sign in another sense also. The sacrifice of our Lord upon the cross was a sacrifice to end all propitiatory sacrifices. There was no further use for the Temple, even for the inner shrine of the Holy of Holies which symbolized the very presence of God. Christ offered one sacrifice to last for ever and then— sat down! And sat down at the right hand of God, never again to suffer (Heb. 10:12–14). Henceforth the temple of God's habitation is the heart of his believing people (Eph. 2:21–22). We may now contrast Matthew 23:21. God used the Roman power to show us in bricks and mortar—or in their absence —that his gospel is now let loose in the world. The benefits of the one sacrifice which took place on one historic spot are now available to every man in every place.

We have outlined the growth of the Roman Empire and from our review have learned something of the nature of this great historical phenomenon to which the gospel first came. It was a world very much unlike our own world of today. To begin, it had not two thousand years of Christian history behind it. There was a startling newness about the Christian faith. Its doctrines were unheard of and its divinities foreign, Jesus and Anastasis (Resurrection, Acts 17:18–20). It may be said that in this post-Christian age in which we live the

gospel is equally strange, and there is much truth in the as-
sertion. Ignorant young men have stood in the dock and
admitted that they had never heard the name of God or
Jesus, except in expletives. Even theological students in inter-
denominational conference have heard of the new birth for
the first time. We are constantly being told that in the West
we have a mission field on our doorstep.

All these are facts which we ignore at our peril. There is
much ignorance, even among the educated. But it is not quite
the same as the ignorance of the first century. At that time
men did not know of the gospel because they had never been
told. It had not even existed. Today men do not know, but
they have been told nevertheless. This does not of course
mean that everybody has been to a church service or attended an evangelistic meeting or even read the Bible. It does
mean that Christianity has made its lasting impact on history and left its traces far and wide.

The secular historian cannot ignore it. He may disbelieve
its doctrines, lack faith in our Lord Jesus Christ and be
devoid of that understanding of its inner meaning which
comes to the believer. But a Gibbon or a Bury, even an
agnostic or an enemy of the faith, if he is an honest historian,
has to take account of his data. He cannot be blind to broad
movements in history; to controversies and their settlement;
to revivals and their consequences; to prominent men and
their influence; to the effect of the wide reading of the King
James Version in literature and life; and even to the buildings, some centuries old and some of comparatively recent
erection. Some of the great triumphs of architecture are to
the glory of Jesus Christ. Some of the very names tell their
story. St. Paul, Minnesota—who and what was St. Paul? Los
Angeles—what does the term mean? San Francisco—what is
a "San" and what is the tale of "Francisco"? St. Petersburg,
Petrograd, Leningrad—how are we to account for the change
of name? What is it that has been officially rejected?

All these are pieces of evidence which the historian cannot
neglect and the educated person should not neglect, if he is
to be really educated. But the ancient world to which the
gospel came had none of these things. It was only after the

sustained preaching of the gospel that they became available. But once they are available, they must be considered. That is why Edward Gibbon (1737–94) could begin the fifteenth chapter (a famous chapter!) of his celebrated *Decline and Fall of the Roman Empire* with these words: "A candid but rational inquiry into the progress and establishment of Christianity may be considered as a very essential part of the history of the Roman empire."

The ancient world did not have the evidence. It was a world unlike our own.

It was unlike our own in another sense also. There is indeed much apathy today, and indifference to the Christian faith. In some places the church may have a bad press, or no press at all by simply being ignored. But its Master still lives and men will not leave him alone. Broadcasters blaspheme and the authorities do not stop them. Entertainers mock and the crowd laughs. Historic scenes are parodied, doctrines distorted and absurdities are wickedly invented. The sacred is secularized and fortunes are made in the process. It would all be quite impossible apart from the abiding effect of the gospel in the world. In the very early days the preaching of the good news might encounter hostility or even riots in this city or in that; objection might be taken to men who upset the world and speak of "another King, Jesus" (Acts 17:6–7); but it was a local complaint. It could not at this stage be otherwise. The great impact had yet to be made.

The object of evangelism of the primitive church, namely the world of its day, was different from ours politically. It was one world, gathered round the Mediterranean Sea. There were certainly other territories: the Far East of India and China and the deep South of Africa. There was contact with India but it was a remote land, a supplier of some goods for trade but living its own separate life. These vast continents had not yet entered the main stream of history. The "ancient world" was one, and under one government.

And the government rested on the army, commanded by one man in civil republican dress indeed but with a uniform, so to speak, which he could don at any time if necessary. But the inhabitants of the empire did not have to toe the party line as if they lived in that other land of one government, the modern Russia. Rome was tolerant of what was cherished in the varied localities under her rule: local laws and institutions, social habits and customs, economic and religious practices, differences of language and cultural tradition. Men were not brainwashed or subjected to incessant propaganda from the monolithic state. As long as they recognized and did not betray the one authority under the umbrella of whose law they lived, they enjoyed considerable freedom. The constituent elements of the empire, the varied provinces and peoples, lived together in the Augustan peace—and lived their own lives.

It is not so with us. We have no Augustan peace and the United Nations are far from united and do not rule the world. Some advocate world government and argue that the logic of the situation demands it. But men are not always led by logic and it is far from realization—if it ever comes. However strong the arguments they are no match for the emotional power of patriotism and nationalism. Men talk of world government—and the Scots and the Welsh demonstrate for a local parliament, and in Canada some noisy people in the province of Quebec seek political and financial suicide by "separation" from the rest of the country.

The ancient world differed from ours in a broad social sense. We have referred to Rome's toleration of different languages. They did indeed exist and were used; but at the same time there was one universal language. As a result of the conquests of Alexander the Great (356–323 B.C.), both military and cultural, the different Greek dialects were fused on one "common" or koinē Greek, which by Roman times had spread over the Mediterranean lands. It had its literary form, but inscriptions and papyri show that the koinē had become the language of the common man. Paul could preach and be understood in Greek up in the hinterland of Asia in Lystra and not himself know the local vernacular (Acts 14:11; cf. 21:37, 40), and in Jerusalem he could address his compatriots in their own language and a Roman officer in

Greek. He wrote his letter to the Romans, not in Latin, but in Greek.

We have not yet reached this stage in the modern world. English is widely known and has replaced French as the language of diplomacy. But in West Berlin I have heard Dr. Graham preach in English and reach the crowds through a German interpreter. There is no reason to suppose that a traveling evangelist would get far in Europe if he confined himself to English. Even in North America there are members of ethnic groups who do not yet speak English.

The ancient world had the medium of communication, a common language, but its means were appallingly slow. They had no airlines, railways or even automobiles. Far from having atomic-powered ships, they lacked both oil and steam. They relied on the oar and sail. They had no satellites to facilitate transmission, no television or radio, no telephone and no telegraph. They had no computer to "do the work" but they did have a large supply of slaves.

The state instituted no national—or imperial—system of education and at the other extreme tolerated an unrefined delight in cruelty and bloodshed. The fighting of gladiators in public shows is notorious, with the spectators' "thumbs up" to deny mercy to the wounded. Sometimes men fought with animals, and at times pity was felt for the animals. Bloodthirstiness increased under the empire. In its earlier days thousands of elephants were killed for the pleasure of the crowd.

Elephants seem far removed from the modern world, certainly the world of the West. No doubt they are used in India for ceremonial purposes and in other less colorful ways. We meet them in Roman history in the army, where they were used in imitation of other nations, though never in an important role. Hannibal started off from Spain to invade Italy and in spite of enormous difficulty and loss managed to bring some elephants through the Alps. They could be used as baggage animals or in fighting if well enough handled to prevent their taking alarm.

It is a long way from elephants to rockets. But the "baggage" which they carried reminds us of all the impedimenta of an army; and in fighting they may have been nearer to invulnerability than the horse. Problems of "logistics" sound very up to date. The need of some sort of protection is still with us. The ancient elephant in the army may well be the precursor of the cargo airplane and the military tank. The Romans share with us the headaches of logistics and protection. They are more like us than we may have realized.

For in spite of all that we have hitherto seen, they were like us. It can hardly be doubted that they reacted to the word *taxes* in much the same way as we do. Travel was comparatively safe and restrictions few. We have our highroads and turnpikes, and our air routes. They had a network of roads and an open sea and some regular sailings. Men could travel for business purposes and a Roman firm could have branches in Greece. Trade and industry suffered no interference from the state—a free enterprise system. There was not a bank at every street intersection as we should understand it, but there was a banking system: financial business with wide ramifications, "risk" capital and rates of interest, letters of credit, and of course imports and exports and the like.

The institution of slavery—hideous in itself yet an improvement on "no quarter" when victory in war is assured—meant a large supply of cheap labor. The slave was an animated tool or a detachable limb and merely had to be kept alive and in working condition. The poor free men were undercut. This partly explains the drift to the cities. The wealthy enjoyed their "summer homes," but the love of the rural scene was not in their hearts. The city was their home and center where they found society with all its gossip and animation. The world from their day up to the end of the eighteenth century could have taken lessons from them in the art of "gracious living." Surrounded by beautiful public buildings and artificial street lighting at night, they knew the amenities of paved streets, drainage, something like indoor plumbing and central heating by hot air. The rootless and the displaced—modern enough!—sought company in clubs, and there was intermingling of men of diverse origins. Perhaps the "American melting-pot" was casting its shadow backwards. The wealthy had their own circle of friends and no domestic servant problem.

Roman society was divided by class and not by caste. As with us, there was class mobility. A slave might be emancipated, a free man might obtain the citizenship. A man might go up in the world. The ascent might not be "from log cabin to White House," but there were such beings as the *nouveaux riches.* But wealth and ease, though widespread, did not come to the humblest. Their enjoyment took another form.

The proletariat was diverted by a succession of shows and spectacles, arranged under the authority of what in at least one country today is called the "Minister of Sport." In earlier days it had found its heroes—or entertainers—in politicians or generals. Now they actually watched them in the arena, "rooting" for their favorite gladiator or charioteer. A generation has arisen which has transferred its enthusiasm from men like Stonewall Jackson or Ulysses Grant to a leading football, baseball or hockey player. The age of the "star" began earlier than we realize.

General morals were not high. The stage was hardly a refining influence. Gossip, slander and gambling were rife. Divorce was easy and our "consecutive polygamy" not unknown. "Thou hast had five husbands; and he whom thou now hast is not thy husband" (John 4:18, KJV). Unwanted babies were exposed, on a hillside or other lonely spot, to be devoured by wild animals or to be picked up by human brutes for the traffic in foundlings who were later to staff the brothels. We may not expose babies today, but we follow the ancient lead in attacking them earlier. Abortion was common at every Greek and Roman level. With us it has become a racket.

As with us, religion had decayed. Thinking men had little regard for it; moral philosophers objected that the gods were not squeamish: their conduct was worse than that of men. In the consequent vacuum there was a restlessness and fever, a lack of satisfaction. Traveling "preachers" could get a crowd to listen to their diatribes, and men with all sorts of quack remedies offered their wares to a credulous public.

Astrology, witchcraft and the occult caught the attention of the superstitious. "New" religions caught on. California was born.

One dominant religion was the cult of the emperor. It may or may not have satisfied some yearning of the heart, but it was a political test of loyalty. We saw something of the same thing in the attitude of Hitler.

The treatment of the dead reminds us of our common mortality. Both burial and cremation were practiced. The ancients were men of like passions with us. They and we are alike in our human nature. In the Roman empire as in the modern world there were all sorts and conditions of men, but they were still men, just as we are still men. They loved and hated. They enjoyed their pleasure and endured—or succumbed to—their pain. They knew the joys and sorrows of life. Marriage and parenthood could mean everything to them, or nothing. Men could care for their wives and children, or neglect them. There could be faithful spouses, and adultery. The callous could look into the grave and not care less; others in sorrow could wish they shared the grave. Cicero could break his heart over the death of his daughter Tullia and be offended by her stepmother's lack of sympathy —and finally divorce her.

Not only in the family but outside it there was good and bad feeling, friendship and hostility. Men were linked in political alignment with their "party" fellows and clashed in bitter enmity with their opponents. They could be selfish or helpful as the case might be. They would go to all lengths to seek revenge or to help a friend. Instant violence might be the order of the day, or secret plots would look to a future when they would reach their consummation in some vile deed.

Ambition played its part in individuals and in the state. It could become voracious and insatiable. Then, as now, men were moved by the love of money and the pleasure of exercising power and rule over others. Some would reveal an enthusiasm which almost rose to frenzy, and would sacrifice much in order to gain more. Others might watch their careers with detachment, uninterested in their pursuits. The

cunning and the guileless may at times have met. Some
showed contempt and some gave their praise; some were
jealous and hid their envy in their desire to overreach the
others.

Men varied then as now in their knowledge. Some had
little that was worth the name of knowledge and others had
cultivated minds. Some were philosophic and others unre-
flective. By and large the Greeks were the philosophers and
the Romans the practical men, the men of law, the engineers.
T. R. Glover used to draw attention to the presence of drains
in Rome and their absence in Athens. The Greeks studied
geometry for its own sake, because they enjoyed it: the
Egyptians attended to it to help them in real estate! By the
time of the Roman empire Greek philosophy had fallen from
its high estate, though St. Paul could encounter Stoics and
Epicureans in Athens (Acts 17:18). Rome never had a thinker
of the eminence of Plato or Aristotle, who have divided
posterity into Platonists and Aristotelians, though Seneca
and Marcus Aurelius have exercised considerable influence.
Lucretius with his atoms strikes a modern note.

Knowledge is one thing, as with Claudius, and wisdom another, of which perhaps Augustus may be taken as an example. There is a wisdom which pertains to life in general and
a practical wisdom which may appear as political insight or
as little more than low cunning. The race of such is not yet
dead. At the other extreme we see separate acts of folly or
a congenital stupidity. Men could be experienced, and learn
from their experience; and they could be inexperienced all
their lives. They could be mature, some from quite early
days, and others immature whatever happened to them.
Poise and self-consciousness rubbed shoulders with each
other. Brilliance could sparkle before their fellows' eyes or
dullness could have all the force of a sleeping tablet. Men
were quick and slow, impatient in their reactions or ponder-
ous in their immobility. They would race through life like a
deer or shamble along like a bear or an elephant. The con-
servatives loved the old and trusted ways and the radicals
would "try anything once." The old wine was better and attracted some; to others novelty always made its appeal.

Friendship could be restricted but friendliness range far afield. Some could repel with class-consciousness, snobbish to the fingertips and arrogant in word and deed. A gradually rising tide of humanitarianism might gently wash the rocks of hardship. Men were short-sighted or far-sighted; wore blinkers or recognized in some measure the forces of history. Their policy, in public state or private life, could be deliberate or improvised, the result of calculation or of impulse. They could act according to principle or from expediency. They might be idealists or realists. Some might live in a world of dreams or in an Aristophanic cloud-cuckoo-town and some devise practical means to achieve a very worldly goal. They knew achievement and disappointment, success and failure. Some would persist and some vacillate, and some do both in alternation. They could hope and despair, be resolute or weak-kneed. Bravery among them is not sought in vain, and even foolhardiness in enterprise. Cowardliness is not absent in the crisis, and timidity in spirit. Decent people could be shocked at outrageous conduct; and sordidness would not come amiss to others. Men would work and seek amusement by turns. Frivolity could strike a people like a plague; and at intervals solemnity steal over them. Noble characters could be found; and some could be corrupted by the possession and abuse of slaves, and by the consequent satisfaction of their slightest whim; and could live to see their own children corrupted by the evil influence of the obedient and indulgent slave.

It is clear that the world to which the gospel came was a world of human beings not unlike ourselves. Their flesh and blood was of the very stuff of human nature, and human nature has not changed. The change has come to the means, not to those who use the means. We take an automobile or an airplane; they took a horse or a ship. We press a switch and the room is flooded with light; they lit a candle or a lamp. They used swords; we use flame-throwers or—in hope and prayer let us say "we do not use"—intercontinental-ballistic-missiles. How little we have changed: the Romans had a *ballista*, a machine for projectiles. Our machines are just a bit more sophisticated.

War is still the "continuation of policy by other means," to adapt Karl von Clausewitz's phrase. It is still the imposition by force of one will over another. And politics is still in a broad sense the relation of the rulers and the ruled. We still seek pleasure, the psychological feeling of which remains the same. We still try to avoid pain, both physical pain and mental agony, though the feeling has not changed. Our amenities are greater in number and perhaps better.

If the gospel was relevant in the first century, it is relevant now.

It may be argued that nothing which comes out of a period so long ago can possibly have anything to do with us, even if our human nature is but the ancient human nature in new clothes. This is often said but it is not true to life.

During a university lecture I once heard a professor state that "the man who invented the figure 'nought' [zero] was a mathematical genius." That must have been long ago, but we still use the figure zero. It is very relevant to our decimal system.

During World War II Winston Churchill at one stage said in his engaging manner: "Under a treaty with Portugal of thirteen hundred and . . . we have occupied the Azores." What was done six centuries earlier was still relevant. If we must refer to time, we can say that the gospel has worn well. It is still the power of God unto salvation. But it not only stands the test of time; it can be examined—and pass the examination.

We might notice that people of earlier days asked some of the same questions as we do or at any rate had the same burden on their minds. Disaster strikes, bloodshed or the fall of a massive building, and people are injured or killed. To what purpose? Do you think that the sufferers were sinners more than anyone else? See Luke 13:1–5. And when he who has the answers is speaking to men, then, as now, they let their attention wander to their own affairs and private interests. When our Lord was addressing the crowds on matters of eternal importance, one of them shouted out: "Tell my brother to divide the inheritance with me." When he should have been listening to the sermon, he was thinking about a family feud over a will (Luke 12:13). This might have happened on Main Street last week.

The ancients were like us supremely in this: they were sinners. And it is to them that the gospel is directed. "Christ Jesus came into the world to save sinners" (1 Tim. 1:15).

2.

The Gospel

THE CHRISTIAN FAITH in general and the gospel in particular
is not merely a system, an intellectual construction of doctrines, coherent and awe-inspiring though it is. It is a remedy
to meet a situation. It is "the power of God for the purpose
of salvation" (Rom. 1:16) and salvation is sorely needed by
men. We must first therefore consider the situation which
God's remedy, the gospel, is designed to meet.

Note the word "designed." The gospel did not merely
"happen." It is not the result of some lucky chance. It is
not haphazard or an example of "muddling through." God
planned it in advance and acted in accordance with his plan.
"God did not send his Son into the world in order that he
might judge the world but in order that the world might be
saved through him" (John 3:17). Here is the evidence of
purpose, both negative and positive; the rejection of one
plan and the adoption of another.

We live in an age of planning. Some countries have a
Ministry of Town Planning. What started as no more than a
field appears five years later as a thriving community. We
see everything in its place: Town Hall, Post Office, Fire
Station, Hospital, shopping center, churches and schools
and all the rest. They are in their most convenient position
because it was all thought out in advance.

We speak similarly of family planning. Children are born
to parents from time to time, "spaced out" at intervals to
help the mother and conform to the family budget. We hear

35

much, especially in some troubled or socialist areas, of economic planning. It is not always successful and economists are not always agreed on what is the best plan. But they agree on the desirability of planning. Such expressions as "Five Year Plan" have become well known.

The idea of a divine plan therefore ought not to trouble us. We should be ready for it and take it in our stride. It is just another instance—though the most important one of all—of what we have all around us in our daily lives. The divine plan is like a human plan in the fact that it is a plan but it differs in its scale and range. It began in eternity, was implemented and continues to be implemented in history, and will reach its climax in a future eternity. It is a remedy and we must first ask ourselves what it sought to remedy.

The Situation Which the Gospel Is Designed to Meet

All men are sinners. There is no exception to this universal statement, apart from him in whom was no sin. When we speak of "man," we mean every person on the face of the earth.

Man as creature thinks and acts as if he were the creator. He is God-less. He may or may not accept the fact that God exists. If God does not exist, it does not matter; if he does exist, that is just too bad—for God. For men live in a practical disregard of him and suppress the truth by the way in which they live. If they feel some desire to worship, they abandon God's truth in exchange for falsehood, and worship and serve the creature to the neglect of the Creator (Rom. 1:18, 25).

In actual fact man is utterly dependent on God for his existence and subsistence. Apart from God as Creator man would not be here. Apart from God's continued blessings he would lack food and shelter and all that he needs to live. "God who made the world and everything in it and is Lord of heaven and earth . . . is not tended by human hands in his need of anything. He himself gives to all—life and breath and everything" (Acts 17:24–25).

Man chooses not to recognize his need. In spite of Harvest

Thanksgivings—or crop failures—he acts as if he were independent and self-sufficient. His behavior suggests that he can be the source of his own supply. His attitude is not the commercial "You want it? We have it"—a not unpleasing form of advertisement. It is rather "I want it. I can supply it." He looks out on creation as if it were his own, forgetting that "the earth and all that is in it belongs to the Lord" (1 Cor. 10:26). He takes what he wants. His standard is his own enjoyment, "the pleasures of sin," temporary though they are (Heb. 11:25).

Man as creature acts as if he were the Creator: as dependent, he acts as if he were independent and self-sufficient. It is in this spirit that man rejects his duty. He is under obligation but he acts as if he were free from obligation. He has some knowledge of God because God himself has made it available: anybody can see it—the fact that God is God and has eternal power. But man chooses to ignore it, giving God neither glory nor thanksgiving (Rom. 1:19-21). God's demands on men are written in the law, which the Jews possess, and in the hearts of the Gentiles, who were not given the law (Rom. 2:14-15). Jews "set aside" the law from their attention (Heb. 10:28), abandoning God's commandment in favor of human tradition (Mark 7:8-9) in consequence of their "setting it aside." They ignore it, reject it, abandon it. Gentiles exulted in breaking free from the claims of law, only to find—if they would but admit it—that they had reduced themselves to a new bondage. They had made themselves—as they still do—slaves to lawlessness (Rom. 6:19).

The requirements of the law, written in a book or in the heart, are fulfilled in the life of love. "Thou shalt love thy neighbor as thyself. Love does no harm to the neighbor. Therefore love is the fulfillment of the law" (Rom. 13:8-10). Prior to the law of loving one's neighbor is the first and great commandment, "Thou shalt love the Lord thy God with all thy heart and with all thy soul and with all thy mind and with all thy strength" (Matt. 22:37-40; Mark 12:28-31, KJV). We have already seen that man does not love God. He is God-less. Does he love his neighbor?

To some extent it may be said that he does. St. Paul spoke of Gentiles carrying out the demands of the law by nature, though they do not possess the law (Rom. 2:14). Our Lord recognized that men, though evil, give good gifts to their children (Luke 11:13). But on the whole man's love of neighbor is feeble and unenthusiastic. If it is effective it is "secular." He does not love his fellow men because God commands him to do so. He does not say, "We love, because he first loved us" (1 John 4:19). He may love indeed: even sinners love those who love them (Luke 6:32).

Thus not all sinners are "gross" sinners. Not all are drunkards, wife-beaters, thieves or crooks. A proportion are moral derelicts, but others are civic models who give good service to their community or are good neighbors to the man next door. Thus there are virtuous sinners. Those whose daily lives are spent in the company of others with whom they work may have greater opportunities for entanglement and temptation, for provocation and anger. Those who work with things rather than with persons and are more isolated may feel less of the stress of life.

Virtuous or vicious, the God-less sinner reveals himself by his absorption in his own activities and interests. We might think that the men who perished in the Flood in Noah's time were wicked enough (Gen. 6:5–7). But notice how our Lord saw and understood their wickedness. "They were eating, they were drinking, they were marrying and they were being given in marriage, until the day on which Noah entered into the ark, and the flood came and destroyed them all." It was similar with the men of Sodom (Gen. 18:20; 19:15, 24). Our Lord said that "they were eating, they were drinking, they were buying, they were selling, they were planting, they were building" (Luke 17:26–29). All these activities seem innocent enough. But the Lord rained fire and brimstone from heaven and destroyed them all.

Wherein were they sinning? Are eating, marrying, business, agriculture and construction of buildings to be regarded as wrong and wicked, deserving of fearful penalty? Of course not: the sinfulness consisted in the concentration. The men were absorbed in it all—in forgetfulness of God. There is a modern ring about this. How many businessmen have been urged, "Don't make business your God"?

The essence of sin is self, sometimes regarded as pride. The sinner is like a man who has been lent a summer home by a friend. It was understood that he was welcome to all its amenities for two or three weeks, but he stayed on and on, refusing to leave and finally trying to establish "squatter's rights." The sinner is like a chauffeur who refuses to drive where he is directed and finally goes off with the automobile and never returns. He is like the manager of a business who so manipulates its affairs in general and its finances in particular that in the end he gains complete control and ownership. He is like a military man who is both in and under authority and who in time of war raises his own disloyalty to a principle and deserts to the other side.

Man is thus a rebel whose attitude and disobedience challenges God's right to rule him. He is an idolator who withholds from God the worship, thanksgiving and service which God is worthy to receive and who takes his orders from another source—himself. He is a cad who bites the hand that feeds him. His spite is well illustrated in Dean Samuel Crossman's hymn, "My song is love unknown," in the stanza concerning the crowd at the cross:

> Why, what hath my Lord done?
>   What makes this rage and spite?
> He made the lame to run,
>   He gave the blind their sight.
>   Sweet injuries!
>   Yet they at these
>   Themselves displease,
>   And 'gainst Him rise.

Sweet injuries! How blest is man and how sourly he responds! Rebel, idolator, traitor, cad: the fine clothes in which he dresses, and the brilliant social life which he leads, the helpfulness to the neighbor and the civic benefactions which he makes, all of them fail to disguise the sordid squalor of his mind. He is in the world and without God (Eph. 2:12) and without hope—and he loves to have it so.

He is distant from God—and loves the distance. He is dead in trespasses and sins (Eph. 2:1)—and revels in it.

This is one side of the "situation." On the other side stands God himself. What does he think of it all? This depends on his identity and character.

There is one God and one only. We must not think that there are many divine beings with our God superior to them all. There are "gods" indeed, recognized by men, but they have no divine existence at all (1 Cor. 8:4–6). There is but one God. He is the living God (Heb. 3:12), eternal (Rom. 1:20; 16:26) and invisible (John 1:18).

He is thus more than a mere principle, the great first cause or the ground of the universe. He is conscious, for he remembers and has knowledge (Heb. 6:10; 2 Tim. 2:19) and wisdom (1 Cor. 1:18–25). But it is not an impotent knowledge and wisdom like that of a scientist held up by lack of financial grants from the government, a doctor with an assured answer to a new disease or a politician of insight with a sound suggestion—and nobody will listen. God has power: he created the universe and keeps it in being (Rom. 11:36; 1 Cor. 8:6). He has will ("Thy will be done") and the long term will which is purpose (Eph. 1:11). His purpose is flexible and he may change his treatment of men, but he does not change his mind and does not lie (Heb. 6:17–18). He is righteous (Rom. 1:17) and trustworthy (1 Cor. 10:13), and he requires righteousness from men (Rom. 6:18–19). He is holy (1 Pet. 1:15–16), "high and lifted up," and separate in his unutterable moral goodness and perfection. He requires holiness in men and worship from them (Matt. 4:10).

When men prove to be disobedient, rebels, sinners, God observes the fact and is displeased (1 Cor. 10:5; Heb. 11:6). For he has an attitude to them and their deeds. He does not merely observe. He evaluates. As individuals—and he deals with individuals (Heb. 3:12; 4:1, 11; cf. Gal. 4:7)—they are responsible and answerable to him (Rom. 3:19; 14:10–12).

He rightly accuses them, for they have no defense (Rom. 1:20; 2:1; 3:9), and he blames them (Heb. 8:8). The whole situation cries out for him to act *against* them in his displeasure as Judge. "The face of the Lord (his manifest presence) is against those who do evil deeds." "God resists the arrogant" (1 Pet. 3:12; 5:5). Judgment belongs to God alone (Rom. 12:19; Heb. 10:30) and it penetrates all the secrets of every heart (Heb. 4:12). It is deserved and just (Rom. 2:2, 6), inescapable (Heb. 2:2–3), terrifying (Heb. 10:27, 31), final (Matt. 25:46). To the sinner God would say: "You are guilty and must be punished. You are unclean and must not come near me."

All this is true but it is not all of the truth. God is not only the Judge. The New Testament speaks of his long-suffering and forbearance, his kindness and his love. He shows mercy and grace (Rom. 2:4; 5:8; Eph. 2:4–8).

When we think of God's longsuffering we emphasize the "long" rather than the "suffering." He allows time to pass, even though the sinner is working against God's cause and purpose, to give him time to repent. In one sense time means nothing to the eternal God: he can never be too early or too late. But he knows what it means to us who dwell in time. He sees men's follies and sins and—in their scheme of things —he waits.

In his forbearance God still waits but there is an added thought. He does not react to men's sin in immediate counteraction. In a duel the swordsman parries every cut and thrust straightway. When in the ring, a boxer fends off every blow and gets in his uppercut as soon as he can. Tread suddenly on the toes of an ill-tempered man and he may knock you down within a second. God is the very opposite of all this. He "puts up" with men's sins. It is more than merely waiting. It is like an excellent marksman who nevertheless "holds his fire." He does not shoot from the hip. As long as he "forbears" he does not shoot at all.

God's kindness and love can for the moment be left to make their own simple appeal. God's "mercy" means his compassion, his pity. It is not only what he feels but what he does. It shows itself in what we should call acts of kindness. The Good Samaritan came across a man who had been beaten up, stripped and left half dead. He treated and bandaged his wounds and conveyed him to his own hotel for further care. On his departure he committed him to the owner-manager, paid both the accounts up to the very hour, and virtually left an I.O.U. to be settled on his return. This act of unsolicited kindness was "showing mercy" (Luke 10:37).

God acts in such a manner. "Whenever I said 'My foot is slipping'; thy mercy, O Lord, (always) held me up" (Ps. 94:18). Many of us know what it is like to slip suddenly on the smooth ice of an unsanded sidewalk in the depth of winter and when on the point of crashing heavily to feel a strong arm kindly seize us. Many remember the long slip on Skid Row and the divine mercy.

Such mercy shoots up like spring flowers—only it is not limited to spring. It follows us in pursuit all our days. It is around us whichever way we look.

If mercy when we slip is unexpected, grace is both unexpected and against all reasonable anticipation. Mercy for people like that? Impossible! They are beyond pity and they deserve all they get. But divine grace draws near to the graceless and forgives the inexcusable. It is undeserved, unmerited, unearned—free to the ugly bankrupt.

So we seem to have two different pictures of God, his severity and his kindness (Rom. 11:22). He is the Opponent of sinners (though not their enemy) and is *against* them. Yet he would make peace because he is *for* them (Rom. 8:31). He was, is, and always will be, *against* sin. How, then, can he be *for* sinners?

It might be thought that these two attitudes, for and against, are in conflict with each other. They pull in opposite directions like two teams in a tug-of-war. Justice and mercy: which will win in the contest? If justice wins, the last picture which we have of God is that of Judge. What has happened to his love and grace? Was his kindness too feeble? But what if mercy is triumphant? It seems more reassuring but it brings no assurance. A God who could forgive without justice might one day condemn without reason. Justice and mercy need each other.

We have a problem on our hands, the tension between justice and mercy. Judaism felt the burden of it but never solved it. The tension goes right back into the very heart of

God himself. Intent on judgment, God finds that his heart is heavy and turns against him. He is, so to speak, divided in himself (Hosea 11:8). The problem is beyond the solving —by the unaided human mind. But God solved it and he solved it in Christ and in the gospel. We must now therefore turn to the gospel, God's remedy for sin.

The Gospel as Fact

The gospel is no divine afterthought. It is embodied in Jesus Christ our Lord. He is God's eternal Son. "Before Abraham was, I am" (John 8:58); and long before that: through him God made the worlds (Heb. 1:2). St. Paul recognized the secret presence of Christ in Israel's Old Testament history (1 Cor. 10:4). In his eternal existence he was rich but in his grace he became poor for our sake (2 Cor. 8:9) by coming into the world (1 Tim. 1:15; Heb. 10:5). He thus came "from heaven" (1 Cor. 15:47).

God's grace was manifested ("anyone can see it") through the appearing of our Savior Christ Jesus (2 Tim. 1:10). We also read that the grace of God appeared with a saving remedy for all men (Titus 2:11) and that the kindness and love of God our Savior appeared (Titus 3:4). Christ appeared; the grace of God appeared. There are not two appearances. As we have said, Christ himself is the embodiment of the gospel.

Our Lord came into the world because he was sent by the Father (John 8:42; 17:3). He is therefore the Sent One, the Apostle (Heb. 3:1). He was sent to fulfill the divine purpose of salvation (John 3:17). This is expanded in the statement that he was sent for the purpose of our redemption and adoption (Gal. 4:4-5). The two activities are not identical but must be kept quite distinct from each other, distinct yet related. Adoption depends on redemption.

When the Lord came into the world he became incarnate, human (Rom. 1:3; 8:3; 9:5; Heb. 2:8-18; 5:7-8; 1 John 1:1-4; 4:2). He became man without ceasing to be God. We see him in history as Jesus of Nazareth. He was obedient (Rom. 5:19; Phil. 2:8; Heb. 5:8; 10:9) and sinless (Heb. 4:15; 7:26-27).

He was crucified, and on the cross he died. He endured real suffering and it was once and once for all (Heb. 9:25–28; 1 Pet. 3:18).

His death was God's will. The treachery and cruelty which led to the cross, the consummation of human freedom's wickedness (John 19:10–11), was under the control—not the inspiration—of the precise (not general and vague) will and foreknowledge of God (Acts 2:23). God knew in advance, and willed, that his Son should die.

His death was not merely his passion, that fearful experience of "being at the receiving end," of "having something done to him." It was his own voluntary act. "He gave himself for our sins." He is the Son of God who "loved me and delivered himself up for me" (Gal. 1:4; 2:20). "He offered up himself" (Heb. 7:27). "Jesus . . . in return for the joy which lay before him, endured the cross" (Heb. 12:2).

Thus Father and Son together willed the cross. God "did not spare his own Son but delivered him up for us all" (Rom. 8:32). "My Father loves me because I am laying down my life, in order that I may take it up again. Nobody takes it from me but I am laying it down of myself. I have authority to lay it down and I have authority to take it up again. This commandment I received from my Father" (John 10:17–18).

His death was for others, not for himself. He died for the ungodly. He died for us (Rom. 5:6, 8). Paul speaks of the Christian brother "for whom Christ died" (Rom. 14:15; cf. 1 Cor. 8:11). But what did he do for us in his death?

He set aside our sin. "He has appeared once for all at the consummation of the ages for the setting aside of sin through his sacrifice" (Heb. 9:26). As long as sin occupies God's attention, as long as it is in the central position in his mind, so long it will affect his treatment of men. But Christ has set it aside from God's attention. This is expressed in another way when Paul says that he obliterated the adverse handwriting which was against us and "has removed it from the midst" (Col. 2:14). The accusation is blotted out and nothing left to remind us of it, or to remind God.

Our Lord was not diverting God's mind from an unpleasant subject to some more pleasant wishful thinking. He set aside the sin of men from the mind of God by actually removing sin. The Lamb of God removed the sin of the world (John 1:29). He was manifested to shift the burden of sins from men (1 John 3:5), and under the new covenant they are taken away (cf. Rom. 11:27). But if he took them away, what did he do with them? Where did he put them?

He shouldered the burden himself. "He was offered once to bear the sins of many" (Heb. 9:28). "He bore our sins himself in his body on the tree" (1 Pet. 2:24). The awful contrast between our Lord and ourselves is vividly brought out by Paul. "Him who knew no sin God made to be sin—for us" (2 Cor. 5:21). In his representative capacity the Sin-bearer becomes a sinner. The sinless, perfect Son of God bore God's judgment on our sins—not his own. We are guilty, responsible, answerable, and our mouth is stopped (Rom. 3:19). It has not been gagged from the outside but paralyzed from within. We have nothing worthy to say in our own defense. Jesus has said it all by assuming responsibility for us. God's "attention" has therefore been diverted from us, because our sin has been removed from us, and concentrated on Jesus who bore it. His cross is his answer, given for us. We need no longer say that God is against us, because in Christ he is "for us." If he no longer levels a charge against us, who of any consequence could possibly accuse us (Rom. 8:31, 33)?

The New Testament describes the death of Christ in two main ways. It was an act of redemption and an act of purification, a sacrifice.

"Christ redeemed us from the curse of the law by becoming a curse for us" (Gal. 3:13), thus fulfilling the prior part of the purpose of the incarnation (Gal. 4:5). We are thus not our own: we were bought for a price; we are slaves under a new Owner (1 Cor. 6:20; 7:23). Even so there are those who deny the Master who bought them (2 Pet. 2:2). Through his redemption our Lord has delivered us from our guilt ("the curse") and its consequences by taking it upon himself.

God in his justice and righteousness is always against sin. He has spoken against it and acted against it in the cross of Christ: he has judged sin, and our Savior has submitted to the judgment. God himself is therefore free, legitimately,

morally and with justice, to forgive sin. He has upheld the
cause of right—his own righteousness and justice—and has
done so demonstrably, so as to continue to be just and to be
the Justifier of the man who believes in Jesus (Rom. 3:26).

The other category is that of purification by a sacrifice
(Heb. 1:3). God in his absolute holiness is separate from
sinners and bids them "keep out," as our notice boards on
government property so elegantly put it. Man was turned out
of paradise and the presence of God (Gen. 3:24), and he cannot return to God as and when he will. We must be holy if
we are to approach God, and the sinner is unholy and therefore disqualified: unholy, unclean, defiled.

By his sacrifice of himself for our sin Christ shed his blood.
This is the one act of purification (Heb. 1:3). The blood,
when sprinkled on the unholy, exercises a sanctifying power.
Unholiness becomes holiness and the defiled is made clean
and pure. This is the newly received qualification to approach
God. "Let us draw near . . ."—which we were not qualified
to do before (Heb. 9:14; 10:12–14, 22). Through Christ we
now have "access" to God (Rom. 5:2; Eph. 2:18; 3:12) which
was previously denied to us.

God in his righteousness has put sinners into the dock. But
their penalty has been paid and he can maintain his righteousness—and pardon them. God in his holiness has put
sinners at a distance. When they are made holy, the holy God
can receive them. They can draw near in confidence.

Through the work of Christ on the cross, forgiveness,
pardon and peace are open to sinners. But they do not possess these blessings yet. They have to be told about them. If
they are not told, they will not know of the gospel of Christ
(Rom. 10:14–17). Even if they are told, they may refuse the
blessing. But they must be told. This leads us naturally to the
next point.

The Gospel as Preached

A generation or two ago a friend of mine paid a courtesy
call on Professor Rudolf Otto (1869–1937) at his home in Germany. The professor had a collection of what in a Roman
Catholic context would have been called "relics," but as he

was a Protestant the name is not really appropriate. In any case they were not all relics in the accepted sense but rather "religious souvenirs." One of them came from the very early days of the Salvation Army in England and resembled a placard generally found on a newsstand. But it did not contain the "latest news" of the secular world. It asked a question, "Where will you spend eternity?" Otto showed it to my friend. He looked at the placard and then at his guest and said in a highly guttural accent, "A very intelligent question."

It is indeed an intelligent question and it draws attention to the fact that the individual human destiny has not yet been finally settled. Here is a man, for instance, on the road to ruin. But he need not be finally lost. If he makes the right decision, he can be saved. But decision about what?

Clearly he must come to a decision about Christ and the gospel. At the present moment he is lost, dead in trespasses and sins. He can be saved; can pass from death to life and have eternal life. "The pittance pay of sin is death, but the free gift of God is eternal life in Christ Jesus our Lord" (Rom. 6:23).

He is not yet saved but he can be saved. He cannot do it himself but Christ can do it. Christ has not done it yet, but he can do it. "He is able to go to the furthest limit in saving those who draw near to God through him, because he is always alive to intercede for them" (Heb. 7:25). He is able to do it, but he will not do it until the man draws near to God through him. When he does thus draw near he will find that the gospel is "the power of God for salvation" (Rom. 1:16).

If the man in question is not told the gospel, he will not respond to its invitation and will stay unsaved. It is clear that in some way the gospel has to be preached to him. We see from the New Testament that arrangements have been made for this to be done. A whole crowd of "preachers" is released from Jerusalem to spread out to the ends of the earth the good news of the gospel, of Christ Jesus our Lord.

What do the "preachers" actually do? They may or may not be preachers as we understand the term but they have something to say and they say it. They converse with the individual, they are irrepressible in the group and some of them address the crowds. They talk, they speak, they proclaim, they herald, they evangelize. The fullness of their heart overflows in speech. They cannot be silent.

By and large they "tell." It may be that on occasion they engage in dialogue. It is possible, even probable, that dialogue passed into argument. It may be that the temperature rose. After all, it has been said that where Paul went the proceedings ended in riot or revival. But the thrust of their speech was to tell. With some it was just spontaneous. Their heart exploded in speech. With others it was a set purpose. Whether with spontaneity or purpose they just "told." They were witnesses.

The late Stanley Jones used to tell a story of his early days as a missionary in India. He went as an advocate, as what the British call a barrister and what Americans call a counselor. He was to argue God's case. It would be infelicitous to say that he was going to "defend" God, but he intended to present God's case—and win it—with his brilliant argument. But he discovered that God did not want him in this role. He did not want him as the brilliant attorney. His work was to be much more humble—and much more effective. God wanted him as a witness.

So the early Christians went out, some addressing the crowds and others just "gossiping the gospel," but all "giving their testimony." That is what they actually did. But what did they say?

Some would find ready listeners at once. Others would "get alongside" their target by speaking briefly about their situation—adversity, perplexity, sorrow, sin. Then they would tell a story, the story of Christ. Notice that they would keep to facts, not fancies, theories or hopes. This is Jesus and this is what he did. They would draw out the implications of the story but emphasize not the implication but the fact: "God introduces his love to us, with this commendation; he recommends it with this evidence; he demonstrates it with this picture; he proves it with this argument; he concentrates all its scattered aspects in this one essential fact—while we were still sinners, Christ died for us" (Rom. 5:8).

They would offer a gift. Would you like it? Would you like it now? You may have forgiveness of sin and eternal life—now. Make up your mind.

Thus they would summon their listeners to decide. They would command them in God's Name to decide in the right way. They would issue a call. What are the people to do? They should believe the story—the statement of fact. They should turn from their sins and renounce them forever. And they should trust Christ, the Christ who "died for our sins" (1 Cor. 15:1–8), and hand themselves over to him. The "evidence' of the witnesses is thus both command and statement. They call for "repentance toward God and faith in our Lord Jesus" on the basis of their story of "the gospel of the grace of God" (Acts 20:21, 24).

What now is the response of the listeners? Some scoff, some postpone decision, some believe (cf. Acts 17:32–34). Those who do not believe remain as they were—apart from one thing. They can never say at the Day of Judgment that "they never had a chance." They did. They heard the gospel—and rejected it.

But there are those who do hear the Word and believe. They do what they have never done before: they start to believe in Christ. They exercise what is sometimes called "first faith." If they are genuine they certainly go on believing in him; but they had to begin. The New Testament clearly recognizes that nobody is born with faith. Faith starts when the gospel is received (Acts 13:7, 12; 14:1). There is an interesting example of "first faith" in Paul's remark that "our salvation is now nearer than when we believed" (Rom. 13:11). This is not of the order of "the sun is now higher in the sky than when we had our breakfast." Breakfast is over long ago. Paul's statement means "when first we believed"—as *The New English Bible* shows. We are not still eating our breakfast but we are still believing. For "first faith" marks the beginning of the Christian life.

We have now to ask what happens when a man by an act of will, of deliberate trust, repents and puts himself into the hands of Christ. This brings us to our final point.

The Gospel as Received

I was once conducting a mission in a church, and as it began on a Sunday evening we started off with the "normal" service. The choir entered the church at the rear and proceeded up the central aisle. As I followed them I noticed that there seemed to be two organists—an unusual sight. The thought struck me: "What will these people be up to next? Two organs indeed, one large and one small!"

I later discovered the actual facts. There was one organ and beside it a piano where a little girl of twelve was "accompanying" the organist and doing it very well. As the hymn tunes were played by the organist, the pianist came in on parallel lines as it were. I had originally thought that someone had invented a "double-barreled" organ with its two parts mechanically connected. I found that organ and piano were quite distinct and separate from each other, though they were played together and in harmony. There was one organ and one piano, separate and apart, but played together.

It is something like this when the gospel is received, only here we have one organ and four pianos. The organ dominates and the pianos accompany, though each piano is quite distinct from the others. The "one organ" which dominates is sometimes called justification by faith, and it "dominates" because all the rest of the Christian life depends on it. A man comes to Christ in his "first faith." Something happens. What is it?

When a man first believes, God does something "in himself." He "thinks" in a certain way. His "thought" may be regarded from two points of view, according to whether the death of Christ is viewed as an act of redemption or a sacrificial act of purification.

Take the act of redemption first. When a man first believes, God counts him as righteous. "A man is justified by faith apart from works of the law." "To him who does not work but believes on him who justifies the God-less man, to him his faith is counted as righteousness" (Rom. 3:28; 4:5). The "counting" is of the same kind as when Paul says that nothing is unclean in itself but that to the man who counts it un-

clean it is unclean (Rom. 14:14). Similarly the temple of the
great goddess Artemis was in danger of being counted as
nothing, though its solidity stared men in the face (cf. Acts
19:27). It is plain that the counting flies in the face of the
facts. Nothing is unclean and therefore this particular thing
is not unclean. Nevertheless it is counted unclean. This great
temple before men's eyes is one of the wonders of the world.
Gaze upon it with admiration. Yet it is likely that it will be
counted—nothing!

A man comes to Christ and has faith in him. He is a guilty
sinner but he is counted guiltless. He is thoroughly unrighteous but he is counted righteous. Who does the counting?

It can only be God, as Paul clearly shows. He speaks of the
man to whom God "counts righteousness" apart from works
(Rom. 4:6). God has been "thinking." It has taken place in
the divine mind.

Consider now what flows from the cross of Christ as a
sacrificial act of purification. When a man first believes in
Jesus, he is sprinkled with Jesus' blood and thereby cleansed,
purified, sanctified (Heb. 9:13–14; 10:22; 12:24; 1 Pet. 1:2).
He is now qualified to draw near to God, because he has been
made holy. He has been set in a consecrated state. He is not
so far, by the bare act of sprinkling, made a better man. He
has just been "qualified." As unholy, he was previously unfit
to approach God; as holy, he is now fit to approach him; but
no moral "change" has taken place within him. It can hardly
be denied that his newly acquired holiness means that God
now regards him as qualified for his presence.

Thus when a man first believes, God counts him as righteous and regards him as qualified for his presence. God
counts; God regards. It all takes place in the divine mind.
God has been "thinking." If this were all, we might never
have known what God thinks. But *at the same time as God
counts and regards . . .* , he does four other things as well.
He "thinks" within himself; but he also acts towards the
newly believing man.

We have likened God's process of thought to the organ
which dominates. His acts may be compared with the four
pianos. The playing of the four different pianos is distinct

from the organ and is not the organ but it goes on with the organ. We therefore turn to the first piano.

The organ plays and dominates: God thinks. The first piano plays with the dominating organ: God acts. What does he do? He actually receives the believing man. This marks the beginning of Christian experience. Justification in itself is not a human experience but a divine process of thought.

A man comes in faith to Christ and Christ receives him (John 6:37–38; Rom. 15:7). In coming to Christ, he finds that he has come to God, and God has received him (Rom. 14:3). This was the experience of men in the days of the early church. It was also their experience "in the days of his flesh." We read in St. Luke's Gospel that the despised, the ostracized and outcasts—tax-collectors and sinners—were drawing near Jesus to listen to him. Grumblings rolled round the circle of Pharisees and scribes. "This man" (or rather the contemptuous "this fellow") "receives sinners and eats with them."

Three parables follow, the Lost Sheep, the Lost Coin and the Lost Son—the Prodigal Son. When the prodigal returned home, his father saw him at a distance and in compassion ran to welcome him and embraced and kissed him. He interrupted his son's confession by turning to his servants and ordering them to bring out the best clothes and shoes for his son and the family ring as well. But that was not enough: they must kill the fatted calf and begin festivities in celebration of the great event. The lost son had been found; the dead was alive again (Luke 15:1–2, 20–24).

This was a reception indeed; and obviously the father ate with the son—as Jesus did with sinners. Now in the parable the father stands for God. It may be inferred that not only is God "like" Jesus and Jesus "like" God but that when Jesus receives a man, God in Christ also receives him. This is what happens when a man comes to Christ. The first piano is playing hard!

Meanwhile what is the contribution of the second piano? God not only receives the new believer. He gives him a new nature, and thus is active within him. This is expressed in a number of figures in the New Testament. God "begets" him (1 Pet. 1:3) and he is "begotten of God" (1 John 5:1). He is born again and born from above (John 3:3–8; cf. Ezek. 36: 25–27; 37:9–10). The "seed" is not the corruptible seed of normal begetting: the new birth is through the Word of God (1 Pet. 1:23), the gospel, given by a human preacher. The Holy Spirit witnesses to the listener, who is thus "born of the Spirit" (John 3:6). He is no longer mere flesh. Within these limits Paul can claim that through the preached gospel he himself begat his Corinthian readers (1 Cor. 4:15; cf. Philem. 10) and even saved them (1 Cor. 9:22; cf. James 5:20). The preacher is but God's agent; the listener who believes is not just the child of his parents or "willed to believe" by the persuasive preacher (though the preacher may exercise suasion) but is "born of God" (John 1:13; cf. James 1:18).

The life of the "born again" is not a mere intensification of his earlier life. It is on a higher plane, not flesh but spirit (John 3:6). Just as the animal is higher than the plant and man higher than the animal, so born again man is higher than plain man—as he was before he was born again. He is committed to a higher life and a higher behavior. He does not sin. He is not at liberty to sin, and he is helped not to sin by the fact that "God's seed remains in him" (1 John 3:9). This suggests a sort of spiritual heredity and the Word of God abiding in him.

Parallel to the contrast of flesh and spirit is that of the old man and the new man (Rom. 6:6; Eph. 4:22–24; Col. 3:9–10). There is a new creation (2 Cor. 5:17; Gal. 6:15; cf. Titus 3:5–6; James 1:18).

Different aspects of the life of the reborn are revealed in the New Testament. He has received illumination to replace his earlier darkness (2 Cor. 4:6; Eph. 1:18; 1 Pet. 2:9). He has received and savored the heavenly gift and knows by experience that the Word of God is good and that God's power has been working in him (Heb. 6:4–5). He has received Christ (Col. 2:6) and the Holy Spirit (Gal. 3:2). He lives in a new home, the kingdom of Christ the Light (Col. 1:13), and thus is under a new rule, for he is now in the territory of grace (Rom. 5:2), no longer sagging and lolling or lying still in death but standing. And he may well stand because he has

been quickened, made alive with Christ (Eph. 2:5; Col. 2:13).
He has been given eternal life (Rom. 6:23; 1 John 5:11–13).
He has come to Christ and found God in him, and Father and
Son make him their dwelling place (John 14:6, 21–23). This
indwelling is mutual, for he dwells in the Father and in the
Son; and this he knows from the gift of the Holy Spirit
(1 John 2:24, 28; 3:24; 4:13–15; 5:20).

The believer is justified and purified: the deep organ
throbs its lasting message. The first piano has a simple theme
—accepted. The second piano has a theme with variations.
The music gathers its strength. We are almost at the beginning of a crescendo.

The third piano seems to translate the mighty notes of the
organ which impress us into a thrilling melody which ap-
peals, and inspires a response. It tells us of God's adoption.

The believer has not always been a child of God. He has
always been God's creature. He became God's child when he
first believed. Full emphasis must be given to the word *became*. He was not a child but he became one. He did not
achieve it, though he has authority for it (John 1:12). He is
not an interloper in God's family. He has the right to be there,
given to him by God.

The New Testament uses the familiar term *adoption*. When
the new believer is adopted by God, it marks the fulfillment
of God's "long-term policy." Its line was laid down long ago
in eternity. God chose us in Christ before the foundation of
the world and destined us for adoption as his children—
through Christ (Eph. 1:4–5). As a logical consequence—not
a chronological one—he "settled" his grace upon us as a
wealthy man may settle money on his children and grand-
children, and it was still in eternity when he did it. His grace
was "given to us in Christ Jesus before eternal ages" (2 Tim.
1:9). To implement his purpose, "God sent forth his Son,
born of a woman, born under the law" (Gal. 4:4–5), with the
twofold object of redeeming those under the law, and thereby
opening up the way for us "to receive the adoption." It is
received through faith in Christ Jesus (Gal. 3:26). Our adoption is thus the very purpose of the incarnation, springing

from the Father's love. We now have a new name; we are
called God's children and so we are (1 John 3:1).

God has not left us in the dark about our new status, and
he has not merely informed us. He has come to us with a
voice. "In proof that you are sons, God sent forth the Spirit
of his Son into our hearts, crying 'Abba, Father'" (Gal.
4:6–7). We hear his voice—no distant one—and know from
his unhushed presence that we are no longer creatures,
servants, slaves, but—sons.

We should notice here that it is the Spirit who cries, even
shouts. He is determined to arrest our attention and join us
to himself in his approach to God. "Abba, Father" is a bi-
lingual reproduction of the beginning of the Lord's Prayer
as recorded by St. Luke (Luke 11:2). The Spirit shouts in our
hearts: "'Abba, Father'; say it! Say it now! You do it! Call
him *Father!* Use the term *Father* when you call upon him."

And the believing man obeys. He also shouts; he also says
"Father." "You received the Spirit of adoption, in whom we
cry, 'Abba, Father'" (Rom. 8:15–16). The Spirit shouts and
we respond. "The Spirit himself witnesses with our spirit
that we are children of God." Charles Wesley puts it beauti-
fully in his hymn, "Thou great mysterious God unknown":

> If now the Witness were in me,
> Would He not testify of Thee
> In Jesus reconciled?
> And should I not with faith draw nigh,
> And boldly Abba, Father! cry,
> And know myself Thy child?

The result is a clear distinctiveness between those who are
the children of God and those who are not. They stand out
against the background of a crooked and perverse generation
(Phil. 2:15). They are the bright stars shining in the world's
dark sky. The difference between light and darkness and sonship and its absence is absolute (2 Cor. 6:14–18). Even so
the world does not recognize us when it sees us (1 John 3:1).
It does not know the Father, and his children appear as no
more than other human beings (John 17:25).

The third piano combines a "guitar effect" with a thrilling melody. If you are "listening to a tune" being played on several different instruments, you can follow them and even hum or whistle in accompaniment. But it is also possible to single out the guitar. You can listen while the melody goes on and yet concentrate on the guitar. It seems very repetitious and the guitarist strums away, "saying the same thing all the time." It is somewhat like this with our third piano. The right hand plays the pleasing melody but the bass is perpetually the same: Abba, Father; Abba, Father; Abba, Father. . . . The right hand tells the story; the left hand drives it home.

The fourth piano celebrates the praise of God for the certainty which he gives to his people who believe. "Through the Holy Spirit given to us, the love of God has been poured out and permeates our hearts" (Rom. 5:5). The love of God is not only "there." It is experienced. We know it and we believe it (1 John 4:16). In another mood or with another character the process is reversed: "we believe and know" (cf. John 6:69). We are loved *in* God the Father (Jude 1). Once we were loved when we were not thus "in" (John 3:16). Now that we are in we can advance yet further. "May the Lord direct your hearts into the love of God" (2 Thess. 3:5; cf. 1 Thess. 3:11). Once in, we can advance further inland. Like immigrants at the port of arrival, we are "in" the country and the whole hinterland awaits our visit. The love of God invites infinite exploration. Our experience of it is deepened and our knowledge of it grows.

For example, we realize that "God is for us" (Rom. 8:31) and we have the solid evidence of our Lord himself to prove it. God did not spare his own Son—for us. He has given us certain promises, by no means trifling in magnitude and value (2 Cor. 6:16–7:1; 2 Pet. 1:4), and " he who promised is faithful" (Heb. 10:23). No trial or adversity, no danger or hostility, nothing in the whole wide creation can separate us from God's love to us in Christ (Rom. 8:35–39).

Such experience and knowledge wears well and can take the strains of our earthly life and pilgrimage. "I am able for everything" cries St. Paul (Phil. 4:13). "To go on living is—

Christ; to die—gain" (Phil. 1:21). "I know him to whom I have committed myself in trust; I am sure that he is able to keep my deposit [i.e., me, 'deposited' with him] until That Day" (2 Tim. 1:12). Stephen, though part of a team which was charged with the supervision of the food supply for needy widows—a sort of ecclesiastical Herbert Hoover—could not stop preaching and was stoned for his faithfulness. At no time did he try to stop the proceedings—as he might have done—by producing evidence of his innocence or arguments in support of it. He suffered the stoning and under its increasing weight he called upon the Lord. "Lord Jesus, receive my spirit." Finally he knelt down and cried with a loud voice (as if shouting "Abba, Father"), "Lord, do not charge this sin to their account." Then he "fell asleep"—a beautiful Christian interpretation of the climax of lynch law (Acts 7:59–60). What Paul showed in word and deed throughout his Christian life, Stephen showed in word and deed at the end of his life. The love of God in Christ fails not. It wears well in the hearts of his people.

There is one word—and experience—which belongs to the certainty which God has given which is strangely rare these days—*boldness*. This must be accepted with all seriousness and with heightened reverence. It does not mean a pally slap-on-the-back approach to God's awe-ful deity. It does mean taking God at his word.

The believing man with the love of God present in his heart has boldness of access to God. He comes with confidence (Eph. 3:12; Heb. 10:19). He has boldness in prayer (Heb. 4:16; 1 John 3:21–22; 5:14–15). He should prepare for boldness at the Parousia, at the Second Advent (1 John 2:28), not for shrinking from him in shame. If the love of God in his heart assures him of his acceptance in justification, he should quietly and confidently expect to have boldness in the Day of Judgment (1 John 4:17; contrast Rev. 6:15–17). Charles Wesley has it (in his hymn, "And can it be"):

> No condemnation now I dread;
>   Jesus, and all in Him, is mine!
> Alive in Him, my living Head,
>   And clothed in righteousness divine,

Bold I approach the eternal throne,
And claim the crown, through Christ my own.

Do not jettison your boldness (Heb. 10:35).

The fourth piano sweeps on in joyous praise, not exactly rivaling the organ itself but blending with it and with the other instruments. Any one, organ or piano, might conceivably have been a solo. But it takes the orchestrated whole to express what happens when a man turns to Christ.

In justification and purification, we learn what God thinks about a man. When he receives a man and accepts him, he acts towards him. When he "begets" him and brings him to the second birth, with all its different aspects; when he adopts him and makes him his child; when he pours out his love into his heart through the Holy Spirit and gives him a blessed certainty: then God acts within him.

God thinks about a man; he acts toward him; and he acts within him. Each of these activities, though distinct from one another, occur together when a man first believes. Any one of them may be singled out and made the object of thought, but they all take place together. The organ and any piano may likewise be singled out and made the object of our thought. But the intention of the composer is realized when they are all played together.

Thus the preached gospel is received and the Christian life begun. It is lived in the fellowship of the believing, worshiping, witnessing and working church, sustained by individual faith and private prayer and inspired by the expectation of the Lord's final epiphany (Titus 2:13).

3.

The Gospels:
Our Lord Establishing the Gospel

IN OUR DISCUSSION of the "one organ and four pianos," we have seen what happens when a man receives the gospel. He receives salvation, for salvation as it is received here and now consists of justification and purification, divine acceptance, regeneration, adoption, and the experience of certainty. This is in principle the salvation which will be enjoyed in all its fullness throughout eternity. The gospel is preached by means of words. The speaker may use varied figures of speech and other illustrations in order to bring pictures before the minds of his listeners. But the words, in the form of intelligent sentences to express coherent thought, are vital. The "pictures" shed light on the words and make their understanding easier.

Now words as words may be nothing or everything. Hard words break no bones but they may break hearts or even start a war. They may bring information to a hard-pressed army which may turn disaster into victory. In the spiritual realm, however, words by themselves are ineffective even though necessary. The speech of a persuasive talker may convince, but it may be followed by an even more convincing address which reverses previous decisions. In Christian preaching the words are blessed by the Holy Spirit with lasting results. But the Holy Spirit is invisible and the words are but audible and intelligible. The gospel is not preached and received without the double influence of speech and Spirit,

but if we had not more than this there would be the danger
of vagueness and distortion of the message.

What started the process of speechmaking? What made
men go out and preach? They did not invent their message.
Where did it come from? It came from the living Christ,
present among men. He is the subject of the preacher's message. Without him there would be no message, nothing for
the Holy Spirit to bless. Every utterance of the gospel,
blessed as it is by the Spirit, has as its foundation the fact of
Christ, here on earth at a certain time and place (Luke 3:1-3,
16, 21), mighty in deed and word (Luke 24:19). He himself is
the foundation, and our four Gospels are the written statement describing the foundation. He is the "place" from which
the preached gospel started. It started earlier indeed. It goes
back to eternity in the mind and heart of God. But it had its
earthly beginning, "the beginning of the gospel of Jesus
Christ" (Mark 1:1).

The Gospels are the record and they give us all that we
need to know. It is plain that not all the story has been told.
The world is not big enough to contain all the necessary
books! (See John 21:25.) A selection has been made and in
the providence of God a wise selection. "Many other signs
Jesus did in the presence of the disciples which have not been
written in this book; but these have been written in order
that you may believe that the Christ, the Son of God, is Jesus,
and that by believing you may have life in his Name" (John
20:30-31).

In his Preface (Luke 1:1-4) Luke has taken us behind the
scenes and shown us something of the process of writing a
gospel. Many men had tried to write one, utilizing the testimony of original eyewitnesses and ministers. But Luke does
not seem to have been satisfied, and therefore set out to write
a narrative which would leave no uncertainty. His historical
standards are high. He aimed at fidelity to the truth: he
"traced," i.e., investigated everything; at comprehensiveness
of scope: he went back to the beginning; and at order and
accuracy of presentation. Order does not have to be chronological in order to remain order. Accuracy is not only working
on the principle that two plus two equals four—accuracy of

fact—but also a certain clarity in writing. Its opposite would be vagueness or "woolliness."

When Luke began his investigation, his process of "tracing," where did he look? It is intrinsically probable that he had talks with the Virgin Mary, who might be more willing to discuss delicate matters with a physician than with others. She could talk to an angel (Luke 1:34) and to a woman (Luke 1:39–40) but otherwise could observe a seemly reticence. A dozen years after the birth of Jesus she could say "your father and I," (Luke 2:48) in accordance with ordinary custom (cf. Luke 3:23, "as it was currently thought").

Luke was something of a traveler, as a companion of the apostle Paul, and he could have met many people valuable for his project. His use of the pronoun "we" betrays his presence at Tyre, Caesarea, Jerusalem and Sidon (Acts 21:3, 8, 17–18; 27:3). When persecution started at the time of Stephen's death, the church of Jerusalem apart from the apostles spilled out from the city (Acts 8:1; 11:19). Either they stayed away permanently or in time they returned to Jerusalem. Luke could well have encountered "witnesses" in or out of Jerusalem whom he could have "cross-examined" or who could have directed him where to find crucial persons. At Caesarea the four daughters of Philip the evangelist (who was one of "the Seven," Acts 6:5; 21:8) could have supplied much useful information, and Luke had two years in which to elicit what he wanted to know (Acts 24:27): Paul was in prison there for this period.

There were women, many of them, who had attended and gained benefit from the Lord's ministry (Luke 8:2–3; 23:49) and had been present at the cross. Joanna, the wife of a steward of Herod's, could supply at least clues from "palace gossip" in addition to her own personal testimony. See also Luke 24:10. Other key figures are Manaen (Acts 13:1), Mnason, a disciple from the beginning (Acts 21:16), and James and his circle (Acts 21:18; cf. 12:17; 15:13). In Jerusalem Luke would have been glad to visit the home of Mary, the mother of John Mark (Acts 12:12; 13:13; 15:37–38). Mark and Luke were together when Paul wrote his Epistle to the Colossians and his Epistle to Philemon (Col. 4:10, 14;

Philem. 24). They would do more than merely discuss the weather.

We cannot prove that there and then Mark showed Luke his Gospel, but from the contents of Luke's Gospel we can draw the reasonably sure inference that Luke used Mark as a sort of quarry from which he drew stones for his Gospel building. In a sense Luke was master of his material: he selected it. In a sense he was its servant: he retained it as the truth.

We can visualize Luke's methods and procedure. He would "trace" some incident in the life of our Lord or some occasion which came to a climax in a striking saying. He would check the information which might be in writing or write a short account himself from those whom he cross-examined. Let us imagine that he wrote each item on—as we should say —a postcard. Scholars refer to the "postcards" as *pericopai*, "clippings." When Luke had accumulated a certain number he would arrange them in some sort of order, much as a philatelist sorts out his postage stamps, adds one to another and so continues until he has completed "the set." In time, different "sets" are joined together.

All three evangelists, Matthew, Mark and Luke, seem to have followed this method. For these Gospels are interlocked (the Fourth Gospel is separate). They resemble one another in having a common plan, a common selection, a common arrangement and common language. They differ in recording different events, in giving different accounts of the same event and in different language. It is widely accepted that Mark's Gospel is prior to the others and that both Matthew and Luke made use of it. Matthew indeed made it his framework, adding supplements from his own private material and from a source which contained many of our Lord's sayings. Luke used this same source in combination with his own material. This was his "set" of "postcards" which he expanded by adding suitable passages from Mark.

Matthew and Luke both begin with separate stories of the birth of Christ, which Mark does not record. Mark gives no genealogical tree. Matthew traces our Lord's human ancestry back to Abraham and Luke to Adam the son of God. John starts in eternity with the Eternal Word and records that the Word "became flesh and dwelt among us."

After the stories of the Nativity, Matthew and Luke join Mark in stories of Jesus' ministry and a long account of the Passion. (The Gospels have been described as a Passion Story with a long introduction.) The Resurrection is recorded, very briefly by Mark, and in greater and separate details by Matthew and Luke.

Some scholars have regarded the "postcards" as early sermons which through repetition have become stereotyped, taking their color from the "pulpit." Others compare the different accounts and try to establish the theology of the evangelist, e.g., Luke. These questions need not now detain us, as we are mainly concerned with the New Testament as we have it and its "taste," which we should enjoy.

The first three Gospels spend much time in Galilee, and John gives us scenes in the south, though this distinction is not absolute. John records long "speeches" of our Lord which differ in style and content from the parables and other sayings in the first three; he also records a succession of "signs." He has been thought to emphasize the deity of Christ; but Christ's humanity is both a fact and a dogma—the Word who became flesh was weary as the result of a journey (John 4:6). In any case, Mark's estimate of Jesus is as high as that of John: Jesus is the Son of God.

Many and varied are the people who appear to us in the Gospels, but even a casual reading will show that the central Figure is Jesus Christ our Lord. He holds the stage and the attention at every point. What impression does he make upon us as we read? What, in fact, is the style of Jesus?

The New Testament tells us that our Lord was "found in fashion as a man" (Phil. 2:8, KJV). This does not mean that he followed human "fashion" as we generally understand the word. As a matter of fact, the Greek word which the apostle Paul used is an elusive one with a long history. It has been used in a social setting, and in a bad sense has been associated with outward show, fine airs and fine manners. If we think of the clothes which people wear, the word *style* is suitable. Tailors and others speak of the "cut" of a coat, and we sometimes say of a person that "he cut a fine figure." There is no reference to measurements or size. A man may be tall or short, fat or thin. Whatever he is, he has a certain way of "carrying" himself, a certain "carriage." He walks in a certain way. When he speaks, we say that he has some kind of an "air." He uses a distinct mode of address. When he stands in our company, he has perhaps an "attitude" which is characteristic, and his face has a normal "expression." As to gesture, a man may make a sweeping bow or merely incline his head.

All this we have summed up in the word *style*. What was the style of Jesus?

On some occasions it can only be described as magnificent. A storm at sea is not the best opportunity for exhibiting the grandeur and magnificence of men. This normally requires a palatial setting and the unobtrusive movement of discreet servants; or a vast parade ground in which a monarch can inspect his men, with all the pomp and circumstance of the military and the splendor of scarlet and gold. But with Jesus there was no need of palace or parade. His magnificence stands out against the gray background of the sea.

Here are frenzied men in desperation. Their Master is asleep and the storm rages. The violent wind howls in their ears. The sea surges as if a succession of earthquakes had committed their tremors to the deep. Wave after wave strikes the boat and, hardy sailors though they are, they see and fear the end. Mighty waves hide the very boat from sight. The sea comes pouring in. Hurled this way and that by the rocking of their craft they call upon their Master.

With prophetic calm he rises. Both wind and wave sink back, not in exhaustion but at his bidding. Nature responds at once in obedience to his slightest word. Calm fell: the winds were restrained; the deep subsided. Air and water were still.

We have all heard stories of mighty potentates who set a team of slaves in swift motion by the bare clapping of their hands. But they were not in rebellion before he intervened! With majestic mien and utter confidence in his own authority and power, Jesus spoke the word of command. The unruly elements yielded at once. He was magnificent.

His style was magnificent in dealing with nature. The same is true in his encounter with men. When a large crowd surged about the door of the house where he was and prevented access to him, the four men with their paralyzed burden dug through the very roof and lowered their friend into the midst of the crowd inside, in the presence of Jesus. How easy it would have been to comment on his strange adventure or to ask after his health! How cautious many of us would have been in the presence of possible critics, the scribes and Pharisees! Our Lord went straight to the point with authority. "Your sins are forgiven."

This is more than the testimony of an experienced Christion or the absolution of the church. In a day which has marked the resurgence of evangelism, it is not hard to imagine a counselor saying to an inquirer who has come forward: "You really do trust Jesus our Savior? You really have repented and turned to him? Then your sins are forgiven." This is the testimony of a ripe Christian experience. If, on the other hand, the absolution is pronounced in church, it is a declaration that if certain conditions are met, certain consequences may be expected. If a man repents and trusts, his sins are forgiven. But in both cases we have a declaration. The one gives a testimony; the other gives an absolution. The one speaks from his heart; the other speaks from the church at large. Both are in a sense testimony, but it is testimony to what Someone else has done.

But when Jesus says that "your sins are forgiven," he does not merely declare it. He actually does it. He does what only God can do. He forgives sins. Men may *declare* that God has forgiven. Only God can do it. And now Jesus, as it were, steps into the place of the living God. And quite rightly, for he is the Son of God. In the words of Charles Wesley's Christmas hymn,

> Veiled in flesh the Godhead see;
> Hail the incarnate Deity.

This is in the grand style and is worthy of the name of magnificence.

Even when our Lord does nothing and says nothing, his style can be the same. At one stage of the proceedings before his death, he was brought before Pilate, the Roman governor. Pilate had become the more alarmed when he heard mention of "Son of God," and he therefore asked Jesus where he had come from. But Jesus gave him no answer. It has been called "an imperial silence." There are times when royalty does not answer the questions of underlings! Once more, even in his silence, we see the grand style. Jesus is magnificent.

But the style is not uniform. The magnificence of royalty and indeed of deity is not always to be seen. At the other extreme, we see the style of the servant, indeed, rightly understood, of the slave. It was because Jesus realized that the Father had put everything into his hands and that he had come forth from God and was going to God, that he took a towel and washed the feet of his disciples. Knowing what he did—we expect the magnificence but—he descended to the lowly. "He humbled himself." He was no slave, but the style of his action was appropriate to the menial task.

All this we may regard as an illustration of the incarnation itself. "Though he was rich, for your sakes he became poor. . . ." For magnificence befits him. Peter, recalling the Transfiguration, speaks of the honor and glory which he received when the Voice came from the magnificent glory. And what did the Voice say? "This is my Son, my Beloved." This, and the whole Transfiguration itself, shows us that Jesus shared the magnificent glory—in later theological language, that he was and is "of one substance with the Father."

The style was lowly in the Garden of Gethsemane. The Beloved Son who shared the magnificent glory of the Father, the Father who according to the Deuteronomist rides upon the heaven and is the magnificent One of the firmament, this Son knelt and prayed "Not my will but thine be done." It was not the magnificent style of heaven nor the humble style of the servant; it was the style of the obedient Son. He shrank from the awe-ful experience of the cross, the place of divine judgment; he shrank from standing in the place of sinners with whom a holy God can have no fellowship; but the Beloved Son for love of his Father as well as for love of sinners overcame his own feelings. The style is neither magnificent nor servile; it is filial.

It is on the cross itself that the style of Jesus is at its most comprehensive. In spite of anything we tend to imagine to the contrary, it was magnificent. It was magnificent in its setting or circumstance. The sun itself seemed to lose its luster and darkness spread over all the scene. The earth quaked and rocks were split. Nature herself was sensitive to what was happening to the Lord of glory—to her own Lord.

And the style was magnificent also in the behavior that was characteristic of royalty. He reigned from the tree. He suffered there indeed; but he reigned. He had said that the hour had come for the Son to be glorified; he had prayed the Father to glorify his Son; and on the cross he reigned in glory. The dying thief prayed to be remembered when Jesus came into his kingdom; and it was as a King that the Lord replied with his promise. "You will be with me in paradise— today." What superb confidence! What royal favor! What magnificence!

But the style was lowly also. "I thirst." Perhaps never since the days at Bethlehem had Jesus been so dependent on human aid. At best it could only be the rough kindness which might relieve in some measure the final agony. But lowlier still we see him. He is alone in the universe. We do not associate a cry of spiritual anguish with magnificence. "My God, my God, why hast thou forsaken me?" It is the opposite of magnificence. In fact, our Lord is wearing the clothes of the sinner. Just as the justified sinner has "put on the Lord Jesus Christ"; just as the righteousness of Christ has been imputed to the believer; so the unrighteousness of sinners has been imputed to Christ; he has "put on"—sinful men. This is the heart of the atonement, and all authentic worship throbs with its remembrance. The *style* then is the cheap cut of the irresponsible; the shoddy and shabby garb of those who have sunk so low that they care not how they look.

But the styles intermingle. There is still the magnificent style of royalty as he proclaims his triumph: "It is finished." And still he has the filial bearing: "Father, into thy hands I commend my spirit." He was indeed "found in fashion as a man." But what a Man!

Such is the style of Jesus. Such is the impression gained

when men turn their gaze upon him. But what if he turns his gaze upon them? What do they learn from the look in his eye?

As a small boy I had a great interest in the eyebrows of one of our sidesmen or ushers. There were two aisles in our church, and the two ushers used to start at the front when they took up the collection, each taking one aisle. Working toward the back of the church, they did not always finish at the same time. One had to wait for the other. Then the two of them walked, each down his own aisle, for the offertory to be placed on the Communion table.

It was important that they should start together, and that is where the eyebrows come in. I used to watch closely every Sunday. The usher on our side would raise his eyebrows. There must have been some answering sign from the other side, for both men would then march sedately to the front, each carrying the offertory which he had "collected." The raised eyebrows seemed to say: "I am ready to start. Are you? Let us go." The man's face tells a story, asks a question, utters an invitation. It is clear that the look on the face is a quick way of sending a message. And so it is with Jesus.

When Peter denied his Lord, he was still speaking when a cock crew. And the Lord swung round and directed his gaze on Peter. We shall never plumb the depths of that look, but at least we can say that it served as a reminder. Peter remembered the previous word of the Lord, warning him against boastfulness and prophesying the denial.

Our Lord once said that the Son could do nothing "of himself." He does not do anything unless he sees the Father doing it. What the Father does, the Son does likewise. I infer that when the Son looks on a man, he is reflecting the Father's look. Even the expression on the Lord's face is suggestive. It is part of that wider activity which may be called "gesture." The twinkle in the eye or the smile on the lips may sometimes mean more than many words.

We must take this further. We do not now see Jesus. His "gestures" are hidden from us. Not until we see him "as he is" shall we see him "face to face." But for us now all the eloquent message of his gesture and expression is summed up in his cross. We must therefore study the looks of Jesus in the light of Calvary. Each of them expresses a certainty and reinforces anything that he says.

There is, to begin with, the look of judgment. In the Parable of the Wicked Husbandmen (Luke 20:9–19) the story is told of a man who put his vineyard into the care of others and then went abroad. When the time came round he sent a servant to get the fruit but the workmen sent him away empty. He sent another who fared no better. They flogged him and treated him with contempt. A third was sent and his blood flowed: they wounded him and turned him out. Finally he sent his son in the hope that he would command respect. But the workmen put their heads together and decided on extreme measures. This was the heir to the estate. Let us kill him and make the property ours.

It was a wicked act which arose out of covetousness supported by a foolish argument. What will the owner do? He will come and destroy the workmen and assign the vineyard to others.

The drift of the parable is plain. God has sent a succession of prophets to Israel, but the fruits of repentance have been withheld and the prophets rejected. Finally God sent his Son —and the crucifixion rears its head. What will God do? "He will give the vineyard to others." As Paul and Barnabas said to the jealous Jews who railed on them with their contradictions, "Since you are thrusting away the Word of God . . . we are turning to the Gentiles."

Our Lord's audience understood quite well what he meant. When he spoke of giving the vineyard to others, an exclamation spontaneously fell from their lips. "Heaven forbid!" But he fixed his eyes on them and asked them the meaning of the scripture: "The stone which the builders rejected has become the head of the corner." That stone is Christ, the keystone of his church; and the builders themselves are rejected. Anyone who falls on the stone will be crushed; if it falls on him, he will be ground to powder.

Here, then, is judgment, and the words which give expression to it are not alone. Their force of impact is increased immeasurably by the look in our Lord's eye. That direct, searching gaze brought into the situation all the solemnity of the Last Judgment.

Secondly, by contrast, the face of Jesus bears the look of love. The story of the rich young ruler (Mark 10:17–31) is familiar. He ran to Jesus, fell on his knees before him and asked what he was to do to inherit eternal life. Jesus begins by reminding him of the "social" commandments, of his duty to his neighbor. The young man claims to have kept them all from his early days. But there is one thing lacking: his duty to God. He must get rid of his idols (in his case, his wealth) and come back and follow Jesus. As he spoke to him, Jesus "fixed his gaze upon him and loved him." The words in cold print might be interpreted as stern and severe. But the loving look dispels that. Jesus is giving more than a human love; it has a depth and a warmth which belongs to the divine. A man must be blinded by his preoccupation not to recognize it. The look turns what might seem to be punishment into opportunity, and loss into gain.

We do not know if any disciple saw the third "look" which we shall consider, but it must have been there. The Seventy returned with joy from their mission, telling the Lord that even the demons were subordinate to them: when they commanded the demons in Jesus' Name, they obeyed. The power of the enemy is undermined, his fortification breached. "I beheld Satan as lightning fall from heaven." The prophetic eye of Jesus sees in the success of his disciples the victory of his own mission. The language is remarkable in its vividness. When lightning strikes it is not slow. Down it comes with instantaneous speed. So Satan hurtles to his ruin.

The crucifixion is still in the future but its outcome is certain. The satanic underlings are already giving way to the apostolic preachers; in the cross their archleader will receive his decisive defeat. And already Jesus sees it all.

The Seventy may have noticed the look in the Lord's eyes when he told them: "I beheld Satan fall. . . ." But the look which he had when first he saw the vision—that must have been reserved for Satan alone. It was the look of victory. Evil is conquered!

Early in the Lord's ministry, two disciples of John the

Baptist were listening to their temporary master as he
pointed to the Lamb of God. They listened to John—and followed Jesus. One of the two, Andrew, found his own brother
Simon and brought him to Jesus, certain that Jesus was the
Messiah. Simon's welcome was assured and his destiny unfolded. Jesus fixed his understanding eyes on him: "You are
Simon . . . you will be called Kephas (Peter)." The words
are clear and confident; the expression is persuasive and convincing.

Anyone can "prophesy" a destiny. Not everyone can convince that what is said is true. Not everyone can so speak
that his words constitute a call. But Simon found it an im-
pelling call. When later many of Jesus' disciples deserted him
and he asked the Twelve if they wanted to leave also, it was
Peter who asked the unanswerable question: "Lord, to whom
shall we go? It's words of eternal life that you have." The
original look in the Lord's eyes had been confirmed by all
that Peter ever found in Jesus. It was the look of invitation.

We have referred to the rich young ruler. After he had gone
away in sorrow, clinging to his idols, the Lord spoke of the
fussiness and the difficulty with which wealthy people enter
the kingdom of God. The disciples were astounded. Who then
can be saved? The rich have surely received God's blessing.
If they cannot be saved, who can? If God blesses but does not
save, what hope is there for men who have not been blessed?
These human impossibilities are not problems to God. Jesus
fixed his eyes on the disciples and told them, "All things are
possible with God."

Anyone can utter a theological platitude. Not everyone can
convince. But the confident look in the Lord's eyes was proof
enough. And as they continued their discipleship and ministry, they saw in the words and deeds of their Master that
their faith was sound. In the later years—after Pentecost—
they found that what the Lord had called their "greater
works" were done in the power of God. But they learned it
first from the eyes of Jesus.

Finally the look of Jesus reveals the possibility of comfort.
The daughter of Jairus, the ruler of the synagogue, was dead.
Why trouble the Master? He is too late. He enters the house

and gazes on the uproar as people weep and wail in grief. Why the upset? Why the weeping? The little girl is not dead but asleep. Swiftly they change their tone. "They laughed him to scorn, knowing that she was dead" (Luke 8:53, KJV). If only they had looked into his eyes as he surveyed the scene. They would have been prepared for the act which confirmed the look. Taking her by the hand, he said, "Talitha cum"— "Little girl, wake up," much as a Jewish mother might have called her child in the morning. If they had looked at his face they would not have laughed in scorn.

The looks of Jesus, then, express judgment, love, victory, invitation and comfort. We cannot see them now, for he is ascended on high. But we have their equivalent. All that Jesus showed us as he gazed upon men is to be seen in the cross.

In the cross we see judgment, the judgment of God; and Jesus bore it. In the cross we see love, the love of God; and Jesus embodied it. In the cross we see victory, the victory of God; and Jesus gained it. In the cross we see an invitation, the invitation of God to sinners; and Jesus gave it. In the cross we see the possibility of comfort, the comfort of God; and Jesus ensured it. For he who died is the Resurrection and the Life, and God raised him from the dead.

Such is the impression when men look upon the style of Jesus. Such is the message received when he looks upon them. But why should such attention be directed towards him, central Person of the Gospels though he is? It is because he is the central Person. But why is he the central Person?

It is because he is God's final word to men. We should know nothing of God if God did not disclose himself. He has revealed himself in a succession of events, fragmentary and varied; now he has revealed himself in a new category, that of divine Personality; he has spoken to us "in a Son" (Heb. 1:2). God's revelation of himself in his Son is marked by fullness, oneness and finality.

God revealed himself to some degree before Christ came. He has revealed himself since he came. But the content of any and every revelation of God is included in what he said in his Son. What, we may ask, are these revelations of God?

He has given us the ABC of himself, and still does, in crea-

tion—in the realm of nature and in the universe at large. We
should learn from this that his power is eternal and that he
is indeed God (Rom :19-20). There is enough here to condemn us, but not enough to save us.

God revealed himself in the prophets. These holy men were
in the counsel of God and they interpreted to their fellows
the meaning of his mighty acts. "The Lord God does nothing
without revealing his secret to his servants the prophets"
(Amos 3:7). They declared his Word and his will. They stated
his claims, his promises and his threats. It is sometimes said
that revelation is like a transitive verb: it must be completed
in its object and is not revelation until it is recognized and
acknowledged as such. This seems to go too far. A prophet
might warn, and God's revelation in his words not be recognized. Yet men have been told and are therefore responsible.
A rejected or unrecognized revelation is still revelation.

The prophets uttered their message in word and deed, in
poetry and in prose; they spoke to their times and they spoke
intermittently. Finally God spoke in his Son with a lasting
revelation. In its completeness it consists of his Person,
words and work.

Christ was himself sinless, obeying God's law down to the
last detail and living a perfect human life. He knew not only
about God. He knew God as no human being before or after
has ever known him. And he "gave" him: in technical lan
guage, he mediated God to men—and still does. Draw near to
Christ and you draw near to God. Listen to him and you hear
God speak. Trust him, and you have committed yourself to
God.

In his speech our Lord described the character of God and
set forth his claims on men. He spoke of God's blessed prom
ises and gave his loving warnings. He interpreted his ancient
law in greater and deeper detail and pointed to the inner at
titude as well as the outer act. He gave God's invitation to
sinners and he spoke their forgiveness.

His "work" is manifold. In his miracles he showed in a
certain setting of time and space what God is doing all the
time. He showed his mastery over the world, which is both
God's world and his world. "All that is mine is thine, and

thine is mine" (John 17:10; cf. 16:15). His miracles of healing, of casting out evil spirits and of raising the dead, show
more eloquently than words could ever tell the Father's love
for men. Even his forgiveness—and the Father's forgiveness
in him—was deed rather than word. He gave it, and it was
received and not merely heard. "Go in peace"—with lightened
heart and joyous spirit.

Preeminently on the cross he did his great work. Here was
the supreme demonstration of the love of God. Here he felt
the agony both physical and mental of the suffering which
men inflicted on him. But he not only had something done
to him. He was active in the cross. He not only accepted
judgment; he embraced the divine judgment on human sin.
He acted on God for men, releasing through his cross the
divine pardon of sinners.

If we say that God's revelation continues in Christ, we
must be careful how we express it. For God's revelation is
complete in him. That full revelation is not given again, but
it is received afresh in the reception of the Holy Spirit; in
the hearing and receiving of the preached Word, the gospel
of our salvation; in public and private prayer and worship
wherein Christ crucified, risen and glorified is felt and known
as our Contemporary; in reading the written Word, when
we go back in thought and feeling to the days of his flesh and
find him in power at our side; and at the End it will be universally received in that divine event to which the whole
creation moves, received by some for a resurrection of life
and by others for a resurrection of judgment (John 5:29).
God's revelation in Christ is not "repeated." The promises
will be fulfilled and the warnings carried out. Christ has already told us of judgment and mercy, of justice and grace.
At the End his words will be finally implemented and his
inaugurated kingdom finally established.

There is a passage in the Gospels of Matthew and Luke
which, if read aloud without reference to their source, would
lead many people to think that they had come from the
Fourth Gospel. They are a strong link with which the first
three, interlocking, Gospels are joined to John's Gospel. Matthew's version (Matt. 11:27; cf. Luke 10:22) reads thus: "All

things have been delivered to me by my Father, and nobody knows the Son except the Father, nor does anybody know the Father except the Son and he to whom the Son is willing to reveal him."

It takes a Christ to know God and a Christ to reveal him—and there is but "one Lord Jesus Christ, through whom are all things and we through him" (1 Cor. 8:6). He has indeed revealed him, for "he who has seen me has seen the Father" (John 14:9). If it takes a Christ to know God, it takes a God to know Christ—and there is but "one God." The Person of Christ, to whom everything has been delivered, is so rich and infinite, that only God can know him. These riches are unsearchable, unexplored even by those who have started to explore (Eph. 3:8).

Here is the paradox. Christ, rich and infinite, stands in the presence of men for whose sake he had become poor (2 Cor. 8:9). He had no home or shelter, no pillow save his own breast (Luke 9:58; John 19:30). The infinite One had need to journey and could weary from the effort (John 4:6). The infinite Son of God was—and is—Man. Limited to Israel in the days of his flesh, he has blessed the whole world. It has been well put by the nineteenth-century Oxford philosopher Thomas Hill Green: "It is because Jesus, under limiting conditions, lived a life which is limited to no conditions, and under special circumstances proclaimed a principle which is applicable to all circumstances, that His life and His principle are rightly called absolute."

This statement is illuminating but perhaps difficult to understand, and a story may help. Sir Malcolm Sargent was a great musical conductor, but he once himself performed to a small but highly appreciative audience. After dinner one day he sought to entertain a small child. Collecting the empty glasses, he poured a different quantity of water into each one. Then with a knife he tapped first one glass and then another, making them the notes or strings of his unorthodox instrument. Entrancing music from tableware! Under such limiting conditions, the great musician can produce a melody which can be played anywhere. Similarly the great actor can play Hamlet, if need be, when standing on a barrel, or a great company can enact a Shakespearean play, as I have seen it done, on the terrace in front of the school building—and overcome the contrast of brown, scorched grass in a summer of heat and drought with the colorful coolness of "How lush and lusty the grass looks! how green!" (*The Tempest*, Act 2, sc. 1, line 55).

"Pleased as Man with man to dwell": this is how the hymn describes Jesus. But there are hints, to say the least, in the Gospels that he was more than man. Though man, he is God incarnate, *Deus absconditus*, the hidden God. At his baptism, which took place in spite of the initial hesitation of John the Baptist, he was divinely attested as God's beloved (or "only") Son (Matt. 3:13-17). His first Temptation would have been entirely without point if he had not the power to turn stones into bread (Matt. 4:3). He is Lord of the Sabbath (Mark 2:28)—a frightening claim by any mere man, for it is tampering with one of the living God's commandments (Exod. 20:8-11). The title, Son of Man, means no more than man when addressed to Ezekiel (Ezek. 2:1) and was a convenient mode of referring to himself by Jesus. It had little content when thus used, beyond a pointer to a definite man. But there was another meaning, known to Jesus and later to his believing people, suggested by the prophet Daniel (Dan. 7:13-14). The Son of Man here is to have universal and everlasting sovereignty. Our Lord did not disclose his Messiahship prematurely, to avoid being hailed as no more than an earthly deliverer and imperialist. Hence he used the term as in Ezekiel, to be filled out from Daniel when the time was ripe. (Cf. Mark 14:61-62. We are reminded of Matt. 28:18-20; Luke 1:32-33.) When the rich young ruler had claimed to have done all his duty to man and the situation cried out for him to be told to do his duty to God, our Lord said, "Follow me." This is either the blasphemy of man or the utterance of One who was and is God—to be remembered when interpreting our Lord's previous statement that nobody is good except One, God (Mark 10:17-21).

At the Transfiguration he was again divinely attested and the disciples were told to "listen to him." He is not to share three tabernacles with Moses and Elijah, one each. His deity shone through.

Years ago a treaty of peace was signed in a palace in Vienna. There is a room in the palace with five doors which were constructed in preparation for the occasion. Five royal figures could enter at one and the same moment. Thus ingenious men disposed of the problem of precedence. There could have been no question of "Who goes first?" It is not like this with Jesus. There are not three "doors," one for him, one for Moses and one for Elijah. There is no problem of precedence. Our Lord, with his deity manifest, is not merely superior; he is the "only." Hear him.

At Caesarea he was confessed as the Christ, the Son of the living God (Matt. 16:16). In the story of his passion, he stands out as Master of the situation, not a controlled cog in the machinery of fate or an unsuccessful fugitive from the human hounds who wanted to destroy him. He was raised from the dead in majesty, not appearing in a mist but a clear Figure of the Son of God (Rom. 1:4).

We have spoken of hints and of more than hints. Certain explicit statements make it quite plain that in Jesus we see God himself visible in action.

We should begin by noticing that nobody has seen God. He is invisible (Col. 1:15; 1 Tim. 1:17; Heb. 11:27). "No one has seen God at any time" (John 1:18; 1 John 4:12, 20). But Jesus Christ has seen him. "Not that any one has seen the Father, apart from him who is from God: He has seen the Father" (John 6:46). And he has seen him in action. "The Father loves the Son and shows him everything that he himself is doing." And not only so: he does not merely gaze at the Father. He himself acts and follows the Father's lead. "The Son can do nothing of himself, if he does not see the Father doing something. What he does, the Son also likewise does" (John 5:19–20). In a sense the Son does not do anything at all. He is in the Father and the Father in him; "the Father stays in me and does his works" (John 14:10). It follows that "he who has seen me has seen the Father" (John 14:9) and has seen him in action. "He who gazes at me is gazing at him who sent me" (John 12:45).

What, we may ask, that is characteristic of God do we see in Jesus? First of all, we see creation visible. It is God who is the Creator (Gen: 1:1, 11, 20), but in the miracle of the feeding of the multitude it is Jesus who creates. From five loaves and two fishes he fed thousands. He broke the loaves and divided the fishes—after returning thanks to God—and gave the separate "portions" (as they write on the menu in restaurants) to the disciples to serve to the crowd. How his arm must have ached, someone has exclaimed, at the end of the process! There was more food available at the end of the meal than at the beginning, twelve basketfuls of "portions" —not "fragments"—available for any not yet satisfied. More is supplied than needed: a picture of the divine lavishness.

The creative activity—it could have been nothing less— of Jesus has been admirably summed up in the lines of the hymn:

> 'Twas springtime when He blest the bread
> And harvest when He brake.

God not only created the world but he keeps it going and is Master of all activities (cf. Ps. 107:23-31) and changes in it. He is its Sustainer. But Jesus is its Master also. "Who is this, that both wind and sea obey him?" (Mark 4:41; 6:41-44). In him we see creation visible.

Secondly, in Jesus Christ we see God's holiness. The emphasis here is not God's moral perfection but the divine distance from men. In the vision granted to the prophet Isaiah at his call (Isa. 6:1-3), he "saw the Lord sitting upon a throne, high and exalted." Holiness means the divine separateness from men, which is the picture here.

This was the vision which came to Simon, though it was not a "vision." At the Lord's command—and against his own better judgment—he had launched out into the deep and had made a stupendous catch of fish. The majesty and holiness of Jesus swept over him: the awe-ful distance of the holy Lord. But there he was, two feet away. The agony was too much for Simon. Such holiness, such distance, should be distant. There was only one thing to be done and Simon did it. He fell in fear at the feet of Jesus with the suppliant's cry: "Depart from me, because I am a sinful man, O Lord." Holiness and sinfulness cannot dwell together. Thus God's holiness is visible in Jesus.

God in his holiness has no fellowship with sinful men until they are "qualified" by the blood of Jesus. Even so, he is not so detached from them that the course of history continues quite apart from him. God guides and governs everything that happens in nature and history; both the broad stream of history and the life of the individual man, even including his free choice. He actually offers him a choice (Deut. 30:19). He raises up a deliverer who in his free acts is an unconscious tool of God's purpose (Isa. 45:1, 13). God's controlling purpose works through the freedom of men. He is never in despair at what they will do next in their freedom, and he never reduces their freedom of choice to the obedience of a machine. We cannot see clearly into God's detailed methods, but we can find the concept of "permission" useful.

Take for example the story of Joseph. It is as plain as anything could be that his brothers sold Joseph into Egypt (Gen. 37:27–28; Acts 7:9). He himself recognized the obvious truth (Gen. 45:5; 50:20). But he could still say that "it was not you who sent me here, but God" (Gen. 45:8). God "permitted" the brothers to do what they did.

We can therefore speak, thirdly, of providence visible in the life of our Lord. At his arrest he repudiated armed defense. "Do you think that I cannot make an appeal to my Father—and if I do, he will at once supply me with more than twelve legions of angels?" (Matt. 26:53). He "permitted" the crucifixion to be carried out by the free choice and decision of sinful men—which is precisely what God did. God's will and foreknowledge was precise and clear, not vague; and by that will and foreknowledge the Jewish people delivered up the Lord and brought about his crucifixion and death (Acts 2:23), though they were free in their choice and decision and responsible for their sin. It was God's will, but he did not inspire or still less force the sinful activity. He permitted it—just as Jesus did.

Analogously, our Lord permitted the unclean spirits to enter the Gadarene swine (Mark 5:13).

Fourthly, lawgiving is visible in the life of our Lord. Lawgiving belongs to God. It was God who gave the ten com-

mandments (Exod. 20:1–17). But Jesus gave his own commandments (John 14:15, 21; 15:10) and specifically a new
commandment. "This is my commandment, that you love one
another as I loved you" (John 13:34; 15:12). The "my"
should not be overlooked. Jesus has done what God did.

Redemption is the work of God and, fifthly, we find it
visible in Christ. God's redeeming activity is discernible in
the Old Testament. "I will redeem you with arm out-
stretched" (Exod. 6:6, NEB). "With thy strong arm thou
didst redeem thy people" (Ps. 77:15, NEB). "I have redeemed
you . . . the Lord has redeemed Jacob . . . Thus says the
Lord, your Redeemer . . ." (Isa. 44:21–24).

We find now that our Lord speaks of coming to serve and
"to give his life as a ransom for many" (Matt. 20:28; Mark
10:45). His blood "is shed for many for the forgiveness
of sins" (Matt. 26:28; cf. Mark 14:24; Luke 22:20). In his
baptism he had been "numbered with the transgressors"
(Isa. 53:12, KJV), though he knew no sin and had no need
of repentance or repentance-baptism. On the cross he entered
more deeply into their condition: there he had to fulfill the
same scripture (Luke 22:37). In him we see God's redemption visible.

Forgiveness and salvation depend on redemption, through
which they are "released." It is not surprising, therefore,
to see forgiveness and salvation visible in Christ. This is our
sixth "visibility" in Christ, and again it is the work of God.
"Thou, Lord, art good, and ready to forgive" (Ps. 86:5, KJV),
"Stand still, and see the salvation of the Lord" (Exod. 14:13,
KJV; cf. 2 Chron. 20:17). "Salvation belongs to the Lord"
(Ps. 3:8). And to the woman who had plied her sinful trade
in the city and now anointed his feet, our Lord said: "Your
sins have been forgiven . . . your faith has saved you" (Luke
7:48–50).

In the passage already quoted, where the Father shows
the Son everything that he himself is doing, our Lord proceeds to give an illustration. "Just as the Father raises the
dead and brings them to life, so also the Son gives life to
whom he will" (John 5:21). It follows, seventhly, that in
Christ we have resurrection visible. He is himself the obvious

example of God's activity: God raised him from the dead. But he himself also raised men from the dead. In the presence of lamentation which was to be the prelude of the funeral and in the face of unbelieving scorn, he raised the daughter of Jairus (Matt. 9:25; Mark 5:41–42; Luke 8:54–55). In the presence of almost unbelievable sorrow he had compassion on a desolate mother, a widow who had lost her only son, and it was at the funeral itself. He halted the procession and stopped her tears; he raised the young man and gave him—blessed word—to his mother (Luke 7:11–17). It is recorded that Jesus had come to the city of Nain but that "God had visited his people."

Before the funeral; at the funeral; the series is completed by the event some days after the funeral, when the body had been some days in the tomb ("by this time he is stinking"). In the presence of the unavailing consolation of neighbors, Jesus raised his friend Lazarus (John 11:43) by summoning him to come forth.

Finally, in Jesus Christ we have glory visible. Glory belongs to God and "I will not give my glory unto another" (Isa. 42:8; 48:11). The divine purpose underlying the illness of Lazarus was not to be realized in the bare fact of his death: it was for the glory of God—that through the illness the Son of God might be glorified. The Son was glorified (John 11:4) and men saw "the glory of God" (John 11:40). They saw the glory of the Word made flesh (John 1:14).

There is no story of the Transfiguration in the Fourth Gospel. The glory is present there in other ways. In the Transfiguration Moses and Elijah were seen "in glory," and this proves to be "his glory" which Peter and his companions saw (Luke 9:31–32). It will be revealed at the End when Jesus comes again, but Peter has already seen it (1 Pet. 5:1; cf. 2 Pet. 1:16–18).

Creation, holiness, providence, lawgiving, redemption, forgiveness and salvation, resurrection, glory: all are visible in Christ. We have seen that he is the complete and final revelation of God. We have considered the style of Jesus and the impression which he makes when men look upon him, and the message they receive when he looks upon them. We have seen him as man and as more than man, with deity shining through. Why did he come? What did he set out to do? What was his program?

His program is outlined for us in the scripture which our Lord read aloud in the synagogue at Nazareth. He had come to what we should call his hometown, and following his custom he "went to church on Sunday." He seems to have been asked to "read the lesson" and was handed the book of the prophet Isaiah. Either the lesson that day was very short or Luke has summarized it (Luke 4:17–21). When Jesus had finished, he settled down to preach, and his first words arrested the attention of all. He referred to the prophecy just read. "This text has today been fulfilled as you heard it." The Spirit of the Lord is upon him, because he has been anointed (has been "Christed," perhaps a veiled reference to his Messiahship) and he has been sent. The purpose of his coming, his "program," is then outlined.

He is to "preach the gospel to the poor." This suggests that he has something for those who cannot get anything. If they could get something, they would not remain poor. He has a gift for them. It is good news, the gospel. We can hardly fail to be reminded of Paul's statement of our Lord's grace: "though he was rich, for your sakes he became poor, in order that you by his poverty might be made rich" (2 Cor. 8:9). Now the gospel depends on the cross. All that had been written about Jesus in the Old Testament had to be fulfilled. There was a divine necessity that certain events should take place in a definite order. He had to suffer and to rise from the dead on the third day. In his Name repentance leading to the forgiveness of sins had to be preached universally. In virtue of the cross, men were to be called to repentance, to abandon their sins, and they would receive the gift of forgiveness.

But when he preached in Nazareth, the cross was still in the future. From this we may draw two inferences. The blessings which Jesus gave during his ministry before the cross were in virtue of the cross yet to take place; and he was inflexibly determined to go to the cross and complete his work (Luke 9:22, 44–45; 12:50; 17:25; 18:31–34; 24:25–

27, 44–47). He did not expect always to be immediately
understood. Even the disciples who were nearest to him
were slow to understand his clear teaching about his destined
sufferings. There would therefore have been no point in telling the people of Nazareth about his coming cross. He offered the blessings!

He has been sent "to preach deliverance to the captives."
He has something for those who cannot go anywhere because
they are in prison or in bonds. They are, as St. Paul puts it,
"in their sins" (1 Cor. 15:17; cf. John 8:21). This means more
than that they still go on sinning. There are past sins with
which they have to reckon. For consider: suppose that ten
or twenty years ago a man committed a murder. He has not
been found out. It is a long time since the deed was done.
It may be, as I have heard a murderer say, that he has
"learned to live with it." He is not constantly thinking about
it. In some sense he has forgotten it. Yet the murder still
clings to him. He is still "in" it. He was—*and is*—the responsible party. It is still true that he, and no other, did it.
The past sin, which in a manner of speaking is over and
done with, is still with him as guilt. This applies to all his
sins, not only murder, up to the present moment. He is still
"in his sins." He is guilty. As a captive he cannot get away
from his guilt. Guilt, like a prison, encloses him; like a chain
or a rope, it binds him.

Now the gospel tells us that Christ died for our sins and
that he bore our sins. The guilt from which men could not
escape has been transferred from sinners to Christ on the
cross. The prison walls have come down. The chain has been
smashed. The rope has been cut. If a man listens to the
preaching, he will learn of this fact and of what he is offered
"in his (Jesus') Name" (Luke 24:47)—the righteousness of
Christ may be transferred to him. If he looks to Christ in
repentance, he who as a captive could not go anywhere can
now take a journey—a short one. He can come to Christ.
In Christ he can come to God. And God accepts and wel-
comes him. A blessed journey!

We must say something about preaching to the captives.
It is very different from an "offer" once made to the coun-

tries of Eastern Europe. "Throw off your shackles and we will give you all economic aid." The gospel of self-help is of no use to occupied and enslaved peoples. Preaching deliverance to the captives must sound a much more hopeful note.

During World War II, a German raider had been sinking merchant ships in the North Atlantic, taking their crews prisoner. No doubt under the necessity to refuel, she had turned for home, with the captive seamen well below decks. Steaming well to the north of the British Isles, she approached Norway. At this point she turned South and, hugging the coast of Norway, made for the home port in the Baltic Sea.

But a squadron of British destroyers had gained intelligence of her movements and an event took place which might well have come out of the old pirate days. A destroyer came alongside the raider; a boarding party leapt on to the enemy deck; cutlass and saber flashed; the crew was overpowered.

Whether the prisoners below decks heard and wondered, I do not know. But when victory had been won, hatchways were opened and sailors went below to find their comrades. A reassuring shout went up. "It's all right, you fellows. The Navy's here!"

That is preaching deliverance to the captives. "The Navy's here!"

Once more: the cross is still in the future. But the Lord is so sure of it that he does not wait. He preaches *aphesis*, deliverance, release, forgiveness.

He has been sent to preach "recovery of sight to the blind." He has something for those who cannot see anything. He will not only do something for them but in them. He has a medication which will take away their woe. "By his stripes you were healed" (1 Pet. 2:24; cf. Isa. 53:5). The "stripes" of the cross are still in the future, but he will not wait to heal. All his literal restoration of sight (cf. Luke 7:22) symbolizes what he will do for the inward man. Saul of Tarsus thus recovered his sight—and was baptized (Acts 9:10-19). Even though now in his exaltation Jesus is crowned with glory and honor, away from us in heaven at the Father's right hand, we can "look away unto Jesus" and "see Jesus"

(Heb. 2:9; 12:2). All that happens to a man wnen he first comes to Jesus is summed up in the word *illuminated* (Heb. 6:4).

Jesus' mission is to "send away the shattered in freedom." He has something for those who cannot do anything. They are not hindered by prison walls or enveloping bonds. Their trouble is within. They are virtually paralyzed. They cannot do; they cannot enjoy. Once more he works within them. Their vigor is renewed and certainty is given to them. In Christ they find that God accepts them; in Christ they are sure of all the divine blessings, sure of the Father's love, sure that they are indeed his children. Could they be other than vigorous, with such a welcome (Luke 15:20–24)? This is ultimately related to the gift and witness of the Spirit (Rom. 5:5; 8:14–16).

Jesus' mission is to "preach the acceptable year of the Lord," that is, to preach the year in which God will accept men. He has something for men who "never had a chance." Opportunity knocks! This is the year of grace. You do not have to wait. Take the gift now. The time of acceptance is the opportunity of acceptance, of very great acceptance. The time is "now" (cf. 2 Cor. 6:2). Recognize what has come your way (Luke 19:44). The "sale"—without money and without price (Isa. 55:1)—is of limited duration. It is possible to say no to God for the last time. Say yes. Say it now. It is your great chance.

Such in outline is the Lord's program. How did it work out as the months of his ministry unfolded and reached their climax in his death and resurrection?

Those who received his gift and took the opportunity of his blessings have "tasted the powers of the coming age" (Heb. 6:5). They have tasted; they have not yet enjoyed the full meal but they have savored its quality and found it good.

The scripture makes a distinction between the coming age, inaugurated by the Last Day or the Day of the Lord, on the one hand, and this age on the other (Matt. 12:32; 2 Tim. 1:12). It is sometimes said that now that Christ has come, the new age, the coming age, has broken into this age. This almost suggests that the future has broken into the present, though it is hard to understand and indeed is probably irrational. The combination now of the two ages seems to imply the following. It was thought that God was going to do something at the End. Well, he has already done it, earlier than expected. But in a sense he has only started: there is more to follow. What was expectation has become possession, and we still have great expectations. In a word, Christ has come—and will come.

There are five main subjects about each of which we can say that it will be and that it already is. It will come, and it is already here.

The first is judgment. In its future reference, judgment may be regarded as a threat hanging over men. "The men of Nineveh will rise up in the judgment with this generation and will condemn it" (Luke 11:32). In the previous verse the same role is given to "the Queen of the South." The interpretation of the Parable of the Tares pictures judgment at "the consummation of the age" (Matt. 13:40). At the last great tribunal, the "sheep" will be separated from the "goats" (Matt. 25:32). The very day has been fixed by God (Acts 17:31; cf. John 5:28–29). This continues prophetic teaching, as we see from such passages as Isaiah 2:12–22; 13:6, 9–13; Amos 5:18–20; Zephaniah 1:7–18.

But judgment nonetheless is already here. Our Lord did not come to judge, but judgment attends him. "He who does not believe has already been judged" (John 3:18). For judgment is a separation, a dividing of men into two distinct groups, and they do it themselves. The Light has come into the world: some men come to the Light and some do not. On those who do not believe and do not come, the wrath of God abides (John 3:17–21). The wrath of God implements the decision of men. The verdict, already given, is unfavorable.

But there is also a favorable verdict. Some men do come to the Light. All the New Testament teaching about justification by faith involves a picture of a court of law and the dispensation of justice. This is what scholars mean when they say that justification is "forensic." The believer in

Christ has not received the benefit of an amnesty or been "let off." The verdict has been given in his favor. He has been justified. His sins have been blotted out (Acts 3:19; Col. 2:14). There is no condemnation for those who are in Christ Jesus (Rom. 8:1). Believers thus have the Last Judgment behind them. This is indeed a power of the coming age! It is worth observing that our Lord himself used the word *justify*. The repentant publican was justified (Luke 18:9, 14). The pharisee and the publican may be compared with Saul of Tarsus before and after his conversion.

The kingdom of God is likewise both future and present. Every time we pray, "Thy kingdom come" (Matt. 6:10; Luke 11:2), we look forward to the end of history and the beginning of glory. The goal is looked upon as a great banquet. "Many will come from East and West and recline [i.e., 'sit at table'] with Abraham and Isaac and Jacob in the kingdom of Heaven" (Matt. 8:11; cf. Luke 13:28). (From motives of reverence Jews often avoided the Name of God; hence the term, kingdom of heaven.) At the consummation of the age, all ill will be removed and "the righteous will shine as the sun in the kingdom of their Father" (Matt. 13:40–43). Certain ambitions were entertained of sitting one on each side of our Lord in his kingdom (Matt. 20:21) and in his glory (Mark 10:37). He was once questioned by the Pharisees about when the kingdom of God would come (Luke 17:20). On one occasion some people thought that the kingdom of God was about to appear at once (Luke 19:11). It obviously had not dawned yet. The penitent thief prayed to be remembered when Jesus came into his kingdom (Luke 23:42). Joseph of Arimathaea was expecting the kingdom of God (Luke 23:51).

The kingdom was clearly an object of hope and prayer, a kingdom which was eagerly expected but had not yet come. It might be in the near or the distant future, but it was still in the future. On the other hand we read that our Lord preached the gospel of the kingdom (Matt. 4:23; 9:35). He said that "the kingdom of God has come upon you" (Matt. 12:28; Luke 11:20). He also said that "the kingdom of God is within you" (Luke 17:21).

We must be very cautious here. Jesus was addressing Pharisees, some of whom he had severely criticized. We must not so interpret the "within" as if we were equating the kingdom of God with "the religious consciousness" or "the spiritual nature of man." If this were a valid procedure, our Lord need never have come. In our search for the true meaning of "within" it will help us to imagine a scene in the main hall of a great school. The headmaster is speaking to the whole assembled body of students. "I have some excellent news to announce to you. So-and-so has won a brilliant university scholarship. When in the years to come he is a renowned scientist, we shall be proud to recall the days when he was within our ranks."

"Within our ranks" means simply "among us." In the Person of Christ the kingdom of God was embodied. In him it was "among you," even if "you" were Pharisees.

The kingdom of God is not a place but an activity. It means the sovereignty of God, the actual rule of God. It has always existed. God is "a great King over all the earth" (Ps. 47:2). "The Lord has prepared his throne in the heavens; and his kingdom rules over all" (Ps. 103:19). "Thy kingdom is an everlasting kingdom—a kingdom of all ages—and thy dominion endures throughout all generations" (Ps. 145:13; cf. Dan. 4:3, 34). God is "the King of the ages" (1 Tim. 1:17).

This universal and perpetual rule is "over" all. In Christ God rules "among" men, during the days of his flesh. Since Pentecost he has ruled "in" his believing people, for Christ has taken up residence in their hearts (Eph. 3:17). This provides the link with the gospel of the grace of God (Acts 20:24–25). It is through faith that Christ is received into the heart—the Christ of the cross, with all its benefits, benefits of grace, or why should he deign to enter in? He comes as Savior and as King, deliberately, consciously and joyfully received. When he comes in, God comes in. It is because of the gospel of the grace of God that God comes to dwell in hearts such as ours.

The kingdom has clearly "come." It is "righteousness and peace and joy in the Holy Ghost" (Rom. 14:17, KJV). It has come as an opportunity and an offer for all. It has come as a

reality and an experience for me. The powers of the coming
age are certainly working already; and the full glory is still
to come.

Likewise eternal life is both a hope for the future and a
present reality. In the future "many of those who sleep in
the dust of the earth shall awake, some to everlasting life
. . ." (Dan. 12:2). There is nobody who has abandoned
everything for the sake of Christ and the gospel without receiving a hundredfold "now in this time . . . and in the
coming age eternal life" (Mark 10:29–30). "The sons of this
age, people of today, marry and are given in marriage, but
those deemed worthy to experience that age and the resurrection from the dead neither marry nor are given in marriage; for they cannot even die any more, for they are like
angels, and are sons of God because sons of the resurrection.
. . . God is not the God of dead but of living men" (Luke
20:34–38). They all live for him.

But "he who believes in the Son has eternal life" (John
3:36). It does not say "will have." "He who hears my word
and believes him who sent me has eternal life, and does not
come to judgment but has passed from death to life. . . . An
hour is coming *and now is* when the (spiritually) dead will
hear the voice of the Son of God, and those who hear will
live" (John 5:24–25). The Fourth Gospel was written "in
order that you may believe that the Christ, the Son of God,
is Jesus, and that by believing you may have life in his
Name" (John 20:31). Eternal life is to know God and Jesus
Christ (John 17:3). The powers of the future age which will
open up eternal life to believers are already operative to give
them a present enjoyment of it.

If the Holy Spirit is associated with life (cf. Rom. 8:11),
it is not inappropriate that he should be the object of hope
in the same way that life is. The promise of the gift of the
Spirit is vividly given in Joel 2:28–32. The setting is "after-
ward," "the great and the terrible day of the Lord." God
will pour out his Spirit—in the future.

But the long text is quoted by Peter on the Day of Pentecost, and his language is highly significant. "This—the pouring out of the Spirit with the sound like that of a violent

rushing wind, the other manifestations and the result in human behavior—this is that which has been spoken through the prophet Joel: 'And it shall be in the last days, says God, I will pour out . . . ' " (Acts 2:1-4, 14-21). This is that—the last days! The Spirit who was promised for the day of the Lord is here. Expectation has given way to experience. The Spirit is no longer a hope for the future but a present reality. The power of the coming age is mightily at work (cf. Acts 1:8).

Expectation has indeed given way to experience. But it comes back without thrusting experience aside. "We have the first fruits of the Spirit" (Rom. 8:23), the first fruits which consist of the Spirit. "First fruits" implies the second, third and all the rest of the yield which is to follow. The first ears of wheat are signs of the full crop to come. The Holy Spirit is only the beginning: there is "more to come" in our eternal inheritance.

The same thought is conveyed in another picture. God has given us "the earnest of the Spirit" (2 Cor. 1:22; 5:5; Eph. 1:14, KJV). It is the earnest which consists of the Spirit. The gift is "in our hearts," given "to us." "In our hearts" means "to us inwardly, not just in our hands." The "earnest" may be likened to a "down payment" which is a pledge of the full payment later. The original word (*arrhabon*) is used in modern Greek for an engagement ring, the "first installment" of the pledged marriage which is to come.

It might be thought that resurrection can be no more than a hope. As long as we walk the earth we are not in our graves; and to be in the grave is a necessary preliminary to resurrection. It is certainly a sure hope: "I will raise him up at the last day" (John 6:39-40; cf. 5:28-29). "Recompense will be made to you at the resurrection of the righteous" (Luke 14:14).

But Christ himself has been raised! This is no hope but a present reality. A man might argue that "this is his resurrection and not mine," and of course he is right. It can be said that we have been raised with Christ (Col. 2:14; 3:1), but it was "through faith"—which did not exist when Christ was raised. However profound the metaphor is and however

true—and it is true—it is still a metaphor. We have never
been literally in the grave and never literally resurrected.
How then can we bring resurrection into line with the other
"futures" which have become "nows"—judgment, kingdom
of God, eternal life and the gift of the Holy Spirit?

St. Paul shows us the way. He compares Christ with Adam
(Rom. 5:12–21). Now Adam is not a separate, isolated individual. He is a corporation, containing all humanity within
himself. This may be regarded as a biological fact. If believers are "in Christ," he "contains" them within himself. This
is a spiritual fact. They enter into him when they first put
their faith in him.

Christ is never separate from his people. He is distinct
from them: he is Savior and Lord and his people are saved
and servants. But he never leaves them and they are "in"
him.

Now Paul describes our Lord as "risen from the dead, the
first fruits of those who have fallen asleep." He and his people are viewed as "those who have fallen asleep in death." He
is never separate from his people, and in respect of resurrection "what happens to him, happens to them." But it does
not happen at the same time. "Each in his own order": first
Christ and then those who belong to Him—at his appearing
(1 Cor. 15:20–23). He is the first fruits. The rest of the crop
will appear when he appears.

Think of Christ and his people as one long procession.
The procession is out of sight, round the corner of the road,
unseen because in the realm of death. But look! The first
Member of the procession and its Leader has rounded the
corner and has come into full view. He is in sight. The rest
of the procession will come round in due course. But the
resurrection has already started. Christ is raised—the first
fruits (1 Cor. 15:20–24).

The resurrection has already started. Christ has been
raised and his people will certainly be raised when the time
comes. In this sense the future "resurrection of the
righteous" is already present.

The present realities of future expectations can be potent
weapons in the hand of a preacher. Used as questions they

can be rapiers. Do you fear the judgment? Why not come to Christ and leave the judgment behind you? Are you far from the kingdom? Why not enter it now? Have you never seen eternal life? Why not enjoy it now? Are you postponing the day of God's power? Why not ask him for the Holy Spirit (Luke 11:13)? Do you fear the grave? Why not join the procession?

The last words of Jesus on earth have a radiance all their own. "Father, forgive them; they do not know what they do" (Luke 23:34). He was consistent and faithful to the end. He never doubted his Father, even in intense suffering. He lived his creed. His life, and the manner of his leaving it, matched his teaching. He made all allowances for human bias and ignorance. Even at the very cross and in virtue of the cross he interceded for men (cf. 1 John 2:1–2).

To the penitent thief he said: "Today you will be with me in paradise" (Luke 23:43). He reigns in authority from the tree. He answers a prayer. He makes a revelation. He receives a companion. He opens up a refreshing future. His grace is richer than any man's prayer and his answer swifter than our imagination.

Jesus said to his mother: "Woman, behold thy son." To the beloved disciple he said: "Behold thy mother" (John 19: 26–27). "Woman" has not the harshness sometimes associated with it. We should think rather of "Lady"—"Madame" is much too formal. "Lady" would not be inappropriate in addressing a queen.

In dealing with great events and eternal truths we ought not to feel it amiss to turn to simpler themes. Our Lord is concerned with great issues and remembers the smaller details. He can carry out a plan with eternal consequences and give thought to present inconveniences. He bears the sin of all the world and is not unmindful of a woman's sorrow and desolation. He opens the way to heaven itself and makes arrangements for an earthly home. The great love for humanity revealed itself in courtesy, love in the small exchanges of life: "Lady." He might have helped his mother by merely putting her into a home for the elderly; instead he committed her to his disciple's heart. John did not misunderstand the message: he took her to live with him and his. The Lord had given her more than the efficiency of an inn. She now had hearth and home and the love and care of a son. Christ blesses the simplicities of home no less than the stately worship and adoration of our holiest shrine.

After hours on the cross, our Lord shouted with a loud voice: "Eloi, Eloi, lama sabachthani?" This is translated: "My God, my God, why hast thou forsaken me?" (Mark 15: 34, KJV). This is no search for theological information or a doubting of the Father's care. It is a rhetorical question and requires no answer. It is a poignant exclamation of spiritual agony. The holy Son of God was numbered with the transgressors. He was made sin for us, visibly and audibly. If ever he was tempted to come down from the cross and save himself, this was the moment. But he was obedient to the length of death. "And none of the ransomed ever knew how deep were the waters crossed."

"I thirst" (John 19:28). So far our Lord has been concerned with others. He prayed for his persecutors. He encouraged the penitent thief. He made arrangements for his mother. He suffered the ultimate in bearing the sins of the world. Now we have the only word concerned with his own pain. It is precious for what it implies. When the eternal Son of God became man without ceasing to be God, he really did become man. He had a nervous system and an acute sensitiveness. Pain was not just a dull ache but a continuous series of sharp stabs, not concentrated in one point but spread over a wide area. Thirst turned the tenderness of tongue and mouth and throat into sandpaper. Thus he endured and thus he gained forever the ability to sympathize with our weaknesses (Heb. 4:15). He knows them all from the inside; he has experienced them. And he never made the slightest murmur of complaint. While God remained God, he was out of the reach of his rebellious creatures, but when he became man he put himself within their range. See what they did to him when they had the opportunity. The thirst of Christ, a tiny part of the whole suffering of the cross, is a sort of keyhole through which we can see the whole massive work.

"It is finished" (John 19:30). This is no cry of relief that all is over. It is the Victor's shout of triumph. He came into the world with a task to be done, and he did it. The tense of the verb in the Greek is significant—a perfect tense. "It has been brought to completion." His work for men's salvation has been done, without flaw and without omission. Nothing has been forgotten. No part is lacking. The work *is* complete. Salvation *is* available.

Then his work does not need to be done again. It needs no addition and nothing should be taken from it.

"Father, into Thy hands I am entrusting My spirit" (Luke 23:46). At the end of all his suffering, our Lord can still use the word with which he began, "Father." Nothing in all the obedience of his mission dimmed his certainty of the Father's love. He had suffered bitterly in the body. He had known spiritual woe when the Father hid his face from him. But he stepped out into the dark, sure and certain of the Father's welcoming hands. He died alone that his people might never die alone. Friends may escort us to the river's edge but there they have to stop. We pass over—with him. He passed over alone. He is the strong swimmer who carried the rope across, the Pioneer of our salvation (Heb. 2:10).

And God raised him from the dead. We do not here need to dwell upon this fact. We have tasted the Gospels and found them good. We have seen in some measure the Lord establishing the gospel. What exactly did he accomplish?

To begin with, he was sent by the Father and in obedience came down from heaven (cf. John 6:38) and dwelt among us (John 1:14). "Will God dwell with men on the earth?" (1 Kings 8:27; 2 Chron. 6:18). Yes, he can and will and did. This is one of the glories of the Christian faith.

When in 1953 Mount Everest was conquered, two men stood on the top, Edmund Hillary and Tenzing the Sherpa, the great guide and helper. Tenzing scooped up some snow and in the hole thus made left a few items of food: a piece of chocolate, some cookies and some candies. The quantity was not great but the gift was symbolic, an offering to the gods believed to dwell there. Hillary likewise scooped up some snow and deposited a crucifix.

Here is a breathtaking contrast. Do we have to travel to the other side of the world and scale its highest mountain in order to seek God—and then find him invisible? How many of us would and could? In his mercy God himself, in the Person of his Son, has come down to us, visible, audible, tangible (cf. 1 John 1:1–4).

The Son of Man came to seek and to save the lost. This text (Luke 19:10) should always be added to the story of the Prodigal Son (Luke 15:24), to explain why the wanderer had returned.

The seeking and saving involved the life and death of Jesus. He lived a life of perfect obedience and sinlessness. He took no false step, said no wrong word, left nothing undone which should have been done. He was not guilty of a single flaw which would have imperiled our salvation. If he had committed but one sin, the judgment which he bore on the cross would have been in some measure a judgment of his own sin. As it was, he stood under God's judgment for sins which were not his own.

His matchless life was offered in death upon the cross. There he bore the sins of the world. And God accepted his sacrifice, and demonstrated his acceptance by raising him from the dead.

His work was truly done. Never man spake as this Man. He hath done all things well. Redemption was accomplished. It remained for the story to be told among men, for them to share in the benefits of his passion.

4.

The Acts:
The Church Making Known the Gospel

THE BOOK KNOWN AS the Acts of the Apostles resembles the Gospels in at least one point. It is filled with speech and movement. We read of criticisms, charges and mockeries leveled at Christians and of their response. We learn what they said, sometimes in summary form and sometimes in much detail. In general we gain the impression that the Christians have the initiative. They "start it all." They have a story to tell, a message to give. They are determined to give it. Even if they were not so determined and resolute, it seems that the message would bubble up out of them like a spring on the mountainside or a fountain in the park. The pressure is within them, whether they like it or not—and they do not seem to dislike it—and the story must come out. They must talk—or burst.

There is much movement. Men come and go in the streets; they are in and out of the Temple; they go from house to house. They concentrate in one spot or they stream out of the city. They travel by land and by sea and at times the journey is long. They are beset by persecutions and at the mercy of the weather. They gain the hearing of Jews and then are turned out of the synagogue. They are heard with curiosity or with respect, and the hearings end with a polite postponement to another meeting or mockery or even blows. We read of friends and enemies, police and magistrates, high officials of state and "lewd fellows of the baser sort" (Acts 17:5, KJV)—the dregs of the city, marketplace loafers.

There is no central figure. For nearly the first half of the book Peter is in the foreground, and then he gives way to Paul. Peter takes the lead in the early days, and then much space is devoted to the activities of Paul, the great missionary. But neither of them can be regarded as the hero of the tale. And yet there is a central Figure.

The author of the Acts is Luke, and he links the book with his earlier volume, our third Gospel. The first account was devoted to all that "Jesus began to do and to teach" (Acts 1:1). The Acts thus continues the story. It is not, after all, the acts of the apostles which have the prominence. The acts of Jesus dominate the scene. In the Gospels we have seen our Lord establishing the gospel. He spoke it, did it, was it. Now he works through his people in making it known. They have their triumphs and their failures, their joys and sorrows; they are welcomed and they are maligned and persecuted. Their own experiences are little more than circumstances. The theme is the working and the power of the living Christ.

The book begins with a short account of the final meeting of the risen Lord with his apostles before his Ascension. At intervals throughout forty days he had appeared to them, teaching them all about the kingdom of God: an intensive theological course of training in an unusual seminary! He commanded them to wait in Jerusalem for the promised gift of the Holy Spirit. The delay would not be long. The Spirit would come upon them, and with him they would receive power. Then they would spread out to the ends of the earth as witnesses to Christ. They would start in Jerusalem—a sublime example of turning the other cheek.

He ascended majestically in their sight. Visually he was received by a low cloud; spiritually he was exalted to the right hand of God (Acts 2:33). Angelic figures appeared and mingled gentle rebuke with hope and promise. Why stand looking at the sky? The ascended Jesus will come in the same manner as they have seen him go. Meanwhile they returned to Jerusalem to join Mary the mother of Jesus, his brothers and some women. There they obediently settled down to wait—persisting in united prayer. They chose Matthias to replace Judas.

Suddenly they heard what seemed to be the sound of a violent rushing wind. Tongues, apparently of fire, appeared and settled on each of them. They were all filled with the Holy Spirit and began to speak with an utterance given by him. Attracted by the sound, a multitude assembled, astonished at the sight and sound. Peter saw his opportunity and, "supported" by the eleven others, began to speak and "give utterance"—in reliance on his recent gift.

Peter referred to the fulfillment of prophecy, the divine "demonstration" of Jesus and God's plan for his cross and passion. He summoned his hearers, conscience-stricken as they were, to repentance and to baptism in the Name of Jesus Christ. About three thousand received his word, were baptized and were added to the young Christian fellowship. The church was off to a flying start.

There follows a description of activities in Jerusalem: vigorous public preaching, the favor of the populace and the concern of the authorities, arrest and release or escape, and problems which arose in the life of the church. Men were appointed to relieve the apostles of "social work" and one of them, Stephen, though entrusted with the care of needy widows, had also to "preach or burst." He was arrested on a false charge and following a long sermon perished under lynch law, forgiving as he died those who stoned him. Saul of Tarsus took care of the clothes of the witnesses and agreed with what they did.

A great persecution broke out, and the bulk of the church left Jerusalem for Judea and Samaria, "preaching" as they went. Names and incidents are recorded, not least being the conversion of Saul on the road to Damascus. The church reached Galilee. Peter, on tour, appears at Lydda, Joppa and Caesarea. At Caesarea occurred a sort of "Gentile Pentecost." Peter went to Jerusalem to report the conversion of Gentiles and God's acceptance of them. The church continued to spread out and reached Cyprus and Antioch in Syria. Saul was brought to Antioch where with Barnabas he ministered for a full year. Peter at about this time was arrested by King Herod Agrippa I but miraculously escaped. And still the church grew.

In the local church at Antioch the Spirit spoke through prophetic voices, calling for the separation of Barnabas and Saul for what we should call missionary work. They were accordingly recognized as men with a vocation and released from local duty.

They started off on what is traditionally known as St. Paul's first missionary journey. They first made for the island of Cyprus. On disembarking they preached in the synagogues. Heading westward they "combed" the island in their evangelistic work until they came to Paphos. Here an encounter with a Jewish false prophet and sorcerer led to the conversion of the Roman governor, Sergius Paulus, a shrewd man. This helped Luke to show that the Christian faith was politically innocuous.

At this point Saul, also called Paul, seems to take the lead: it is now "Paul and his company." They sail from Paphos to Perga in Pamphylia, on the Southern coast of Asia Minor, the modern Turkey. Here their assistant, John Mark, withdrew from the mission and returned to Jerusalem. They push on into the interior, traveling northward until they reach another Antioch, Antioch in Pisidia. Their ministry in the synagogue was at first welcomed and highly successful, but the vast crowds who came to hear the Word of God did not please the local Jews, and the missionary party had to leave the city. It establishes a pattern: a visit to a synagogue—the obvious "platform" for an itinerant preacher—an initial receptiveness and a believing response, the division of the people into believing and unbelieving, the opposition of the Jews, some persecution, and then a switching from Jews to Gentiles. Paul's watchword was "to the Jew first." When the local Jews finally thrust away the Word of God, and with it eternal life, then "we turn to the Gentiles."

From Antioch they travel in an eastward direction, leaving behind a Christian base from which the Word was spread. They reach Iconium, Lystra and Derbe and the same sort of pattern emerges; preaching, conversions, division, opposition and sometimes downright persecution. At Lystra among the simple country folk Paul performed a miracle of healing. The immediate effect was electrifying. Then the Jews came and stirred up the mob and stoned Paul, dragging him out of the city and believing him to be dead. Paul never forgot the experience. It seems to be the origin of his *stigmata,* the "brand marks of Jesus" (Gal. 6:17).

He nevertheless recovered and retraced his outward route after a visit to Derbe, strengthening and giving encouragement to the new disciples and appointing presbyters or elders for the different churches. After by-passing Cyprus, he and his party reached the original Antioch and reported all that God had done and that he had flung open a door for believing Gentiles to enter.

But the conversion of Gentiles led to a problem. Hardliners, Jewish Christians of the Pharisaic persuasion, came and insisted on obedience to the law of Moses, including circumcision—a serious attack on free grace. Paul and Barnabas and others were in consequence sent for consultation to Jerusalem. At the conference in Jerusalem, often called the Council of Jerusalem, Peter recalled the agelong painful experience of trying to keep the Mosaic law, and God's dealing with the Roman centurion. Paul and Barnabas likewise told their story of God's signs and wonders among the Gentiles. James, the leader of the church in Jerusalem, summed up in terms of the prophetic hope for the Gentiles and gave as his ruling that Gentiles who had turned to God were not to be saddled with the intolerable conditions desired by the rigid Jews. But fellowship in Christ between Jew and Gentile was to be facilitated by discipline in sexuality and abstention in diet from what was abhorrent to Jews. A letter was sent to the Gentile churches conveying the decision and it was received with joy.

Paul and Barnabas stayed for some time in Antioch, working with others in a teaching and evangelistic ministry. But eventually Paul suggested to Barnabas that they should go over their former ground and pay a visit to the churches which they had founded. How were they getting on in the Christian faith and discipleship? Barnabas agreed; but then a problem arose. John Mark had proved unreliable in their former tour but even so Barnabas wanted to include him. Paul dissented: they would have to be "behind" him all the time to push him forward. They could not run the risk of his slipping back to Jerusalem at a crucial moment.

Two men collided head on because of their different standpoints. In a sense, both were right. Barnabas is the kind of man who inspires confidence in younger ministers. They go and "weep on his shoulder," knowing that he understands them and will give them another chance if they have made a grievous mistake. Paul is intent on the missionary task. Nothing must impede the spread of the gospel. There would be hazards enough without adding to them. In the end there were two missionary journeys, not one. Barnabas and Mark took ship for Cyprus. Paul chose Silas, and they traversed Syria and Cilicia in their visitation and encouragement and reached Derbe and Lystra. At Lystra they were joined by a young disciple, Timothy, in their expedition.

An interesting example of divine providence follows. They were prevented by the Holy Spirit from speaking the Word in Asia; and though they tried to travel to Bithynia, the Spirit of Jesus did not permit them. This is surprising: did not Asia and Bithynia need the gospel? But the divine strategy was not in error. Paul was later to have a great ministry in Asia (Acts 19:10), and Peter seems to have been involved in Bithynia (1 Pet. 1:1). At any rate we learn from its governor, Pliny, early in the next century that the province was teeming with Christians.

The missionary party found itself at Troas, near the site of ancient Troy. It was here that Paul had his famous vision in the night: a man of Macedonia stood and urged him, "Come over into Macedonia and help us." *He* saw the vision; but Luke adds, *we* sought to go to Macedonia (Acts 16:9–10). They had "put two and two together" to realize that God had called *us* to evangelism there. They sailed from Troas and landed at the port of Neapolis which served the city of Philippi, ten miles further inland. Thus the gospel gained a foothold in Europe.

Influenced by the message given by Paul, a resident businesswoman, Lydia, opened her heart to the Word and her home to the evangelists. On one occasion when they were out in the city, they met a slave girl who was possessed of some kind of spirit and was used by her owners to do a roaring trade in fortunetelling. She dogged Paul and his friends as they walked along, shouting out, "These men are servants of the Most High God who are proclaiming to you a way of salvation." This daily dose of noisy and unsolicited testimonial was not to the taste of Paul. One day he turned and commanded the spirit in the Name of Jesus Christ to "come out of her." Her owners, in letting her thus roam the street, now received what they had not bargained for. When the spirit "came out," they found that their hope of future profits had "come out" also.

From economic motives the crafty Philippian businessmen dragged Paul and Silas to the authorities and denounced them for uneconomic conduct. Far from mentioning their loss of private profit, they charged them with disturbance of the public peace and, as Jews, advocating un-Roman behavior. The mob took a hand and by official command the two evangelists were stripped, flogged and flung into jail where, in the inner section and with their feet in the stocks, they sang hymns at midnight. A sudden earthquake shook the jail to its foundations. All the doors were instantly opened and chains detached. The jailer woke up, feared the worst and was on the point of suicide when Paul stopped him. The situation led to the classical question and the classical answer: "What must I do to be saved?" "Believe on the Lord Jesus." This swift evangelistic summary of the message should be compared with Paul's other abbreviation, "the word of the cross."

Morning came, but Paul declined to be quietly let out like a cat into the garden. They were Romans! Publicly flogged without even a trial! In fear for their own position, the rulers gave them an escort.

On they went until they arrived at Thessalonica, the modern Salonica. Three sabbath days in the synagogue led to conversions: some Jews, a considerable crowd of pious Greeks and quite a few prominent women. The Jews in jealousy and with the help of roughs roused the city to an uproar and dragged some Christians to the magistrates: they were turning the world upside down and were guilty of sedition. Certainly they were "upsetting" everyone and Jesus is certainly "another king." Friends went bail for the missionaries and sent them off at once by night for Beroea.

In Beroea they made for the synagogue again, there to find a better type of person. The Jews eagerly received the Word and daily examined the scriptures to prove its truth. Many were converted, Jews and Gentiles, men and women. But the Jews in Thessalonica got wind of it and came and staged a demonstration. Leaving Silas and Timothy behind, Paul was conducted by new Christians to Athens.

Here he kicked his heels in frustration, impatiently waiting for his friends and coworkers to come, and appalled at the idols he found when wandering round the city. So much for the glories of Greek sculpture! They meant nothing to a man brought up on the second commandment, with its prohibition of graven images. He argued in the synagogue and daily buttonholed people in the marketplace. He raised the curiosity of some Epicurean and Stoic philosophers and was brought before the venerable Council of the Areopagus for further examination. Such was the city's congenital love of novelty.

Paul took his opportunity and his speech is celebrated. He began in a conciliatory fashion, regarding the Athenians as "rather religious." Their objects of worship were food for thought, especially an altar to an unknown god. This gave him a point of contact. "What you are unknowingly reverencing I am now proclaiming to you." He spoke of the personal God as Creator and as Lord of history and geography, and found support by quoting some of their own authors. From here he went on to the coming judgment, for which God had already appointed a Judge. He has given grounds for belief by raising him from the dead.

This was too much for the audience. As Greeks, they knew all about the immortality of the soul; but the resurrection of the body was distasteful to them—so far were they from the biblical doctrine of personality, the unity of body and soul. Some openly mocked; and the case was otherwise politely and indefinitely adjourned—*sine die*. Even so, believers had been won, including a member of the very council which had examined him. Paul must not be criticized for not preaching the cross: he was not allowed to do so because he was interrupted. Did this influence him in deciding to know nothing but Christ crucified? Possibly; but the cross is not to be thought of as an instrument of one string or the sound of one note. It is a color or a savor which should permeate all doctrine and every sermon.

Paul left Athens and went on to Corinth, where he was intensely active for eighteen months—"absorbed in preaching." The story of his stay in the city has some striking highlights. In the earlier period he reasoned in the synagogue every sabbath day. One source tells us that he "inserted the Name of the Lord Jesus." Think of the possibilities. "Jesus was wounded for our transgressions; Jesus was bruised for our iniquities; the chastisement of our peace was upon Jesus and with his stripes we are healed. . . . The Lord has laid on Jesus the iniquity of us all" (Isa. 53:5–6).

When the resistance of the Jews had gone so far, Paul "went to the Gentiles." He left the synagogue—and set up his headquarters next door! The ruler of the synagogue was himself converted! His whole family came with him and many Corinthians believed and were baptized. The Jews "as one man" swept Paul before Gallio, the governor of the province, as he dispensed justice "on the bench," but since they did not bring a charge of villainy but of religious offences against their law, the governor drove them away. The new ruler of the synagogue was beaten up by the crowd, but the governor did not care a whit.

The governor in question, Gallio, was the brother of Seneca. He is important because an inscription at Delphi which records a proclamation made by the emperor Claudius provides a fixed point for New Testament chronology. Gallio was governor A.D. 51–52, and we can work backward and forward from this date.

A quick visit to Palestine intervenes here, and it may be taken as marking the transition from the second to the third missionary journey. After his travels, we find Paul next at Ephesus.

Here he found some "disciples" who not only had not received the Holy Spirit but did not even know of the Spirit's existence. Inquiry showed that they had received the baptism of John the Baptist. They were then baptized into the Name of the Lord Jesus. When Paul "laid hands" on them, they received the Holy Spirit.

After listening to Paul's bold persuasions in the synagogue for three months, the Jewish mind set like concrete against the message, which was openly reviled. Paul therefore washed his hands of them and "separated" the disciples. It is an old story. "The Jew first" had been given the opportunity and had rejected it. Wider scope than the synagogue was needed. Paul was not taking his converts into a hothouse—except that he hired the lecture hall for the hours when it was not in use, probably from 11:00 A.M. till 4:00 P.M. These were the hottest hours of the day, when most people would be thinking of a siesta. It says much for the apostle's stamina that he could preach and teach every day for two years in such trying conditions. The lecture hall became a center of evangelism from which the gospel radiated throughout the province of Asia. No doubt many people, Jews and heathen, came "up to town" and returned homeward as new Christians and as new, though "amateur," evangelists.

Signs and wonders attended Paul's ministry and he had his imitators. The seven sons of a Jewish "high priest" tried to cast out evil spirits "by the Jesus whom Paul preaches." The reply in one instance was devastating. "Jesus I know and Paul I know, but who are you?" And the possessed man turned on them and drove them out, bare and battered. Thus did the Word of the Lord overcome resistance and loom ever larger. To preach "the Jesus whom Paul preaches" is a good test for an honest man. But every preacher should know the Lord before he enters a pulpit.

Sensational news spread through the city. Fear fell on all, impressed with the Name of the Lord Jesus. Many people collected their valuable occult books and burned them openly. Immersed in his present work Paul could still look and plan ahead, and he had made up his mind that he must see Rome. Then trouble broke out.

Men are sensitive to what touches their pockets, and they

ran true to form in Ephesus. Demetrius, a silversmith, called a meeting of his "union" and set the facts before his fellow craftsmen, who made silver shrines of the goddess Artemis. This fellow Paul has made an impact on the whole province of Asia and is telling people that gods made with human hands are not gods. He must be stopped. Our prosperity is being undermined; our craft is losing its repute. (Note the economic motive.) Further—note the touch of religious respectability—the temple of the great goddess will come to mean nothing and the goddess herself be deprived of her majesty, the goddess of all Asia, worshiped by the world.

The fury of the craftsmen was kindled. The city was reduced to confusion. As one man they rushed to the theater. For two hours there was one united shout, "Great is Artemis of the Ephesians." The situation was ugly.

The town clerk rose to the occasion with soothing and tactful words. Who does not know that the goddess is the patroness of our city? Who can deny that we have evidence to prove it? You must be calm. Don't do anything rash. You have no specific religious offense with which to charge them. If Demetrius and his fellow craftsmen have a grievance against anybody, there are such things as tribunals, and governors to sit on the bench. Take it to court. If you have any further matter to raise, it will be settled at the next meeting of the assembly. We could ourselves have charges hurled at our heads for rioting today without a cause. Off you go—and go quietly.

Paul not long afterwards summoned the Christians for a final message and farewell, and then set out for Macedonia and Greece. After three months there, he foiled a Jewish plot against him by a change of plan. Instead of setting sail for Syria he turned back through Macedonia and reached Troas, Luke now being with him.

Paul shows up in an interesting way at Troas. On the eve of his departure there was a meeting to "break bread," and the apostle, never at a loss for a "sermon," continued speaking until midnight. This may be regarded as the "introduction"! For a youth, sitting on the window ledge, became more and more drowsy and finally "dropped off," lost his balance

and fell from the third story, and was picked up dead. Paul
rushed down and revived him. Up he came, "broke bread,"
and continued preaching until dawn. Then he started out to
walk twenty miles to Assos, to be picked up by the others
who had gone on by ship.

The text, not of the sermon but of the man, could only
be "this one thing I do." Paul was absorbed in his message
and his work, and his dominant interest and purpose gave
wings to both his words and his feet. The "congregation"
obviously loved it—and the preacher. For most of them, the
night was their only free time—and on this occasion the
Word which they drank in was both rest and recreation.

From Assos their ship threaded its way in a southerly
direction until it put in at Miletus. Paul wanted to "sail past
Ephesus"—as he did—and push on to Jerusalem for the Day
of Pentecost. But he sent thirty miles to Ephesus and summoned the presbyters, the elders, of the church there. His
address to them is a classic. It may be doubted if any better
pastoral farewell has ever been uttered. It combines the
authority of the ministry with warm affection; no complacency but an objective review of three years' work; a challenge and warning to the listeners and a self-dedication to
his own dangerous destiny. Certain expressions have become
part of the common language of the church: repentance toward God and faith in our Lord Jesus Christ; the gospel of
the grace of God; the Word of his grace which can build; it
is more blessed to give than to receive.

When he had finished, they all knelt down and prayed.
They wept at the thought of seeing him no more and tenderly
kissed him. Then "they escorted him to the ship."

So he sailed on. He transferred to another ship at Patara
on the South coast of Asia Minor, continued the voyage to
Syria and landed at Tyre. The ship had to unload her cargo
and Paul had seven days with the local disciples. At the end
of the period they all, with wives and children as well, escorted the apostle and his party to the shore, where they
knelt down and prayed with them. The congregation went
home and the missionaries sailed on to Ptolemais for a day
with the local Christians and then to Caesarea for a much

longer stay. Their host was Philip the evangelist, one of "the
seven" earlier appointed with Stephen to look after needy
widows. He had "four virgin daughters who prophesied."

Warnings had been coming through the Holy Spirit all
along the route about the danger which threatened Paul in
Jerusalem, and warning was not lacking in Caesarea. In spite
of his heartbreak at the "opposition," and in readiness for
bonds and even death "for the sake of the Name," Paul
pressed on and arrived in Jerusalem. He and his friends were
warmly received, and his listeners glorified God when they
heard from him in detail what God had done among the
Gentiles through his ministry. By a conciliatory act he
showed that the apostle of free grace and justification by
faith could sympathetically understand his stricter brethren
and without breaking Christian principle follow the custom
of the Old Testament.

But danger was just round the corner. Jews from Asia saw
Paul in the Temple and roused the whole city to a tumult by
going for him and shouting that he had brought Greeks into
the Temple and defiled it. The charge was false but it was
enough to start a blaze. Lynch law was stopped only by the
timely arrival of Roman soldiers and the arrest of Paul. Unable to ascertain the truth because of the din, the commanding officer had him forced through the crowd into the fort; or
rather he ordered it. But finding out that it was a case of
mistaken identity he incredibly gave Paul permission to
address the crowd.

Standing on the steps the apostle waved for silence and
began to speak. His use of the Aramaic produced an even
deeper hush. He touched on his earlier life and then told in
some detail the story of his conversion on the road to
Damascus. All went well until he mentioned his commission
to go to the Gentiles. Then the bomb burst: clothes flying,
dust flung into the air, the crowd clamored for his death.
This time Paul really did get into the fort. He was about to
be examined under torture when the alarmed officer discovered that Paul was a Roman citizen.

Trying to get to the bottom of the matter, the next day the
officer called a meeting of the Sanhedrin, the Jewish chief

court, and confronted them with Paul, allowing him to speak. Paul's immediate reference to his clear conscience before God caused the high priest to command his servants to strike him on the mouth. Paul did not recognize the high priest— possibly because of short sight—and called him a "white-washed wall" (cf. Matt. 23:27). Though true, this hardly helped, though Paul at once admitted his ignorance of the high priest's identity. Then he flung in a brilliant red herring.

Suddenly realizing that the court was made up of both Sadducees and Pharisees, he shouted: "I am a Pharisee and a son of Pharisees. The case turns on our hope of the resurrection of the dead." This split his audience. The Sadducees were skeptics. The Pharisees believed in the resurrection, and some of them rose to make a fight for Paul's innocence. The chasm widened; the uproar grew louder. The commandant feared Paul would be torn in pieces and once more pulled him back into the fort.

There in the night Paul was encouraged. The Lord stood by him: Paul must witness to him in Rome as well as in Jerusalem. And so his trek to Rome started.

Forty Jews and more took an oath not to eat or drink until they had killed Paul. They staged a further investigation, planning his liquidation on his way to it. Paul's nephew got wind of the plot and with his uncle's assistance gained the ear of the commandant.

The officer took swift action. He sent Paul off to Caesarea with an escort of nearly five hundred men, to be examined by Felix, the governor of Syria, in the presence of his accusers. A covering letter calls attention to his Roman citizenship and his innocence, as well as to the Jewish plot.

A formal hearing took place, and Paul had many conversations with the governor, who took fright when he had to listen to talk about righteousness, self-control and coming judgment. Each word hit home. He hoped—in vain—to receive a bribe from Paul, and when his successor arrived after two years, Felix tried to improve his stock with the Jews by leaving the apostle still in custody.

The new governor, Porcius Festus, refused to hear the case in Jerusalem and thus foiled another Jewish plot. A con-

frontation took place in his court in Caesarea, and the Jewish
accusers were not able to prove their case. Festus, not unlike
Felix in his desire to curry favor with Jews, asked if Paul
were willing to be tried before him in Jerusalem. Paul
smelled a rat. He was innocent of the charges, and nobody
could hand him over to his accusers as a present. "I appeal
to Caesar," he demanded.

In an interval before a convenient ship to Rome could be
found, Herod Agrippa II and his sister Bernice paid a visit
to the governor. Festus talked about the recent affair, about
Paul's innocence and his appeal. Agrippa expressed interest,
and the following day Paul was brought in to a scene of great
pomp and circumstance. Festus hardly knew what to say to
Caesar when he sent Paul to Rome: what had the man done?

Paul was permitted to speak and was glad of the chance
to deal with an expert in Jewish affairs. He briefly surveyed
his well-known earlier days which led to his persecution of
Christians. Then again he told of his experience on the road
to Damascus. Some memorable expressions abide. "It is hard
for thee to kick against the pricks." "I was not disobedient
unto the heavenly vision."

The apostle was not to be intimidated. "King Agrippa, do
you believe the prophets? I'm sure you believe them." The
king is evasive. If he repudiates the prophets, he can hardly
be orthodox; if he accepts them, he is dangerously near to
putting himself publicly in Paul's camp. "You're trying to
make me adopt the role of a Christian." Paul has a ready
answer: "Not only you but all these people here. Would that
you were all like me—except these bonds." The VIPs withdrew and agreed on the prisoner's innocence . . . pity he appealed to Caesar.

The Acts goes on to recount the hazardous voyage towards
Rome, the risk taken, the refusal to listen to Paul's good
advice, the great storm and the wreck. After a kindly reception and a three-month, winter stay in the island of Malta,
they boarded another ship and reached Italy, and "thus we
came to Rome." Paul was gladdened by the sight of Roman
Christians at Appii Forum, forty miles or so from the city,
and at Three Taverns (thirty miles or so), who had come to

welcome him. He was not without friends in the church to which he had written a few years earlier. "He thanked God and took courage."

Two local Jewish delegations came to visit him at his own invitation, first the leaders and later many more. He had nothing against his own people—just the hope of Israel, the resurrection, the Messiah and the kingdom of God. One by one some of them believed; others disbelieved. It was the old story in a new setting.

Luke leaves the apostle for a two-year stay in Rome under some form of house-arrest, receiving visitors and preaching and teaching with all boldness and "without let or hindrance."

What has Luke told us in his narrative? The gospel started with a little company of believers in the city of Jerusalem. It moved outward in ever-widening circles until it reached the imperial city itself. It encountered, and overcame, unbelief, opposition, plots and persecution. It made its appeal to simple country folk, to a Roman soldier and to a Roman governor. A single individual can be the object of Christian witness and be converted and baptized; and a whole province can be teeming with Christians. The message is for Jew and Gentile alike and the problem of an increasing number of Gentiles can be met and overcome. The church has been planted and established and a ministry for its pastoral care instituted. Repeated warnings of danger and death have not deterred the apostle to the Gentiles.

Here and there in the account Luke has been at pains to show that Christianity is politically innocuous. Preachers and Christians generally are not revolutionaries. They do not seek to overturn the government or reduce communities to anarchy. In many instances it is the Jews who start the trouble and rouse the populace. In any case the dregs of a city can always be expected to join in vandalism, hooliganism and troublemaking, whatever the issue involved. For Luke, for the preachers and missionaries, and for the church at large, the Master's words carry the final authority: "Render unto Caesar the things that are Caesar's and unto God the things that are God's" (Luke 20:25).

The Lord had said that the disciples would receive power when the Holy Spirit came upon them. Luke has recorded and demonstrated the exercise of the power that certainly came. But how was it exercised? What is most striking when we see it in operation?

In reading the first chapter of the Acts, with its promise of power, a man might be forgiven if he thought that the disciples would wield the power as a weapon. In actual fact they did not spend all their time talking about it or consciously "using" it. They were undoubtedly aware of the possession of power, but far from constantly polishing their weapons they just went right ahead and—preached Christ! Note especially the contrast: they possessed the Spirit but it was Christ whom they preached.

Study of the words and deeds of the disciples will confirm this. The Acts leaves us in no doubt. They were to be witnesses of Jesus, not merely in Jerusalem to begin with, but all the time to the ends of the earth (1:4–8). This was their task and they carried it out (2:32; 10:39). The Holy Spirit himself is witness to Jesus (5:32). He is received by men from Jesus: on his exaltation Jesus received the Spirit from the Father and poured out the gift on the Day of Pentecost (2:33). Ananias was sent by the Lord, Jesus, to the newly converted Saul of Tarsus, "in order that you may be filled with the Holy Spirit" (9:17).

The Holy Spirit is promised to men who have just heard Christ preached, on condition that they repent and are baptized in the Name of Jesus Christ to match the forgiveness of their sins (2:36–39). Believers are disciples, and manifestly disciples of Jesus (5:41–6:2). Stephen was a man full of faith and of the Holy Spirit, and he saw Jesus standing at the right hand of God and it was to Jesus that he prayed as he died (6:5, 14; 7:55–60).

The scattered church told the good news of Jesus, going further and further afield and enlarging their target to include Greeks as well as Jews. Barnabas was sent to Antioch in Syria to investigate the innovation: the "hand," that is, the power, of the Lord was with the speakers and it was to the Lord that a great number who believed turned; Barnabas saw the grace of God and rejoiced, and urged them all to be loyal to the Lord. How are we to explain his attitude and his policy? The Acts says that it was *because* he was a good man and full of the Holy Spirit and faith. A considerable crowd was added to the Lord, and his disciples gained the name of "Christians" (11:19–26; cf. 26:28; 1 Pet. 4:16). It was the Holy Spirit who inspired Barnabas to recognize the activity of the grace of God in the winning of disciples to Jesus. It was to Jesus that the apostles directed the Philippian jailer in the moment of his deepest distress (16:30–31).

When the Holy Spirit is in a believer's heart, what does he do? He points to Jesus. When challenged, Peter was filled with the Holy Spirit and pointed to Jesus as the Healer (4:5–10; cf. Luke 12:12). He pointed to him as the one and only Savior (4:12). He pointed to him as incarnate (4:13; cf. 10:37–47; Mark 3:14). He pointed to him as risen and exalted (2:32–33; cf. 7:55). The Holy Spirit emboldens to speak the Word of God (4:31). He demands truth (5:3, 9) and obedience (7:51). He is needed for the administration of "social welfare" (6:3, 5). He gives vision and inspires prayer and Christlikeness (7:55, 59–60).

The whole Godhead is involved. The Spirit witnesses to Jesus (5:32), Jesus witnesses to the Word of his grace (14:3) and God witnesses by giving the Holy Spirit (15:8–9).

The Holy Spirit is concerned with the ministry, first, before men become ministers. He calls to a ministerial task and he "separates" men for the work to be done (13:2). Jesus had also called men (Mark 1:17, 20), and Paul, a slave of Christ Jesus and an apostle by vocation, was "separated unto the gospel of God" (Rom. 1:1). The Holy Spirit calls, separates and appoints (20:28).

The Holy Spirit is concerned with the ministry, secondly, when men have become ministers. Once in the ministry they find that he directs them. Philip was directed to approach and join the chariot of the Ethiopian eunuch—and he preached Jesus to him (8:29, 35). Peter was directed to go with the servants of Cornelius. It was part of a larger, providential pattern, for the Holy Spirit had sent them (10:19–20; 11:12). Peter obeyed, and when he met Cornelius he preached

Jesus to him (10:34–43). God impartially "accepts" the
serious-minded in every race, but he accepts them as objects
of evangelism; they need to be saved and Peter can show
them how—Jesus! (10:35; 11:14).

The Holy Spirit not only directs. He inspires a resolution
of grace (15:28), a sort of social arrangement which leaves
the gospel intact. He inspires men with a dominant purpose
not immediately to fulfill it but to be guided by his overruling
plan (16:6–7). They travel on, to preach Jesus elsewhere—
already led by the Spirit of Jesus.

The Holy Spirit is linked to the preached Word. While
Peter was still speaking, the Spirit fell on those who were
still listening—and hearkening (10:44). They should be baptized in the Name of Jesus Christ: they had received the Holy
Spirit "just as we did also" (10:46–48). The Holy Spirit is
linked to faith in the Lord Jesus Christ (11:17) and thus to
"first faith." "Did you receive the Holy Spirit when you
started to believe?" (19:2).

To summarize: disciples are disciples of Jesus and they
preach Jesus. God gives them the Holy Spirit and Jesus gives
the Holy Spirit, who is the Spirit of Jesus. The Holy Spirit is
not apart from the Word, the Word which is about Jesus
and is Jesus. Jesus was sent by the Father and the Holy Spirit
witnesses to him. The Father purchased the church—to
which disciples belong—with the blood of Jesus—and this
good news about Jesus is proclaimed in the power of the
Spirit.

The central Figure is Jesus. God himself preaches peace
through him. The Acts of the Apostles is Luke's detailed
record and illustration of the truth of our Lord's words
about the Holy Spirit: "He will glorify me" (John 16:14).

The Acts thus records the continuation of the work of our
Lord. But it is not continuing "to do the same thing." The
Gospels are a preparation for the Acts; the Acts would be
impossible without the Gospels. In the Gospels the materials
are gathered together, the foundation laid. In the Acts the
building begins to rise, built on the foundation, consisting of
the materials.

We may perhaps be able to show the difference between the Gospels and the Acts by the use of our imagination. In the season of Lent many clergymen have been in the habit of preaching a series of sermons on such titles as "Personalities of the Passion." It would be helpful to consider some "Personalities after Pentecost" and to bring the two groups together. At the time of the Passion many people were hostile to our Lord. We shall imagine that their hostility persisted— as with many it undoubtedly did—and let them encounter some appropriate believers from the time after Pentecost. By and large it was the people as a whole which delivered Jesus to death (Acts 3:11-14; cf. John 1:11). Any person or persons singled out from the "people" will thus share the people's guilt.

Now on one occasion the priests—hardly the high priests— were in the company which "came upon" the apostles, arrested them and clapped them in jail for the night (4:1-3). The priests were obviously unbelievers. But the Acts records later that a great crowd of priests was opening the door to the Christian faith (6:7). What would the believing priests say to the unbelieving priests? Or at any rate what could they say?

They could tell them that they had made the biggest mistake of their lives. The crucifixion of Jesus was a misjudgment of fact. Jesus was indeed the expected Messiah. God's promises had been fulfilled in him. They had not got rid of him: God had raised him from the dead. And they had committed a grievous sin. They may have taken no actual part in the crucifixion, but they had supported it. Their own high priests had incited the mob (Mark 15:11)—as disgraceful a procedure for a high priest as for an archbishop—and were there no priests in the crowd to follow their lead? This fearful sin and all their sins could be forgiven. They are offered a gift, here and now. The Lord had told his apostles to begin in Jerusalem. When he was being crucified he had prayed for the forgiveness of his tormentors. Now he again offers pardon.

The priests had much to gain. Their priestly life was a life of drudgery. "You stand performing your ritual duties every

day and offering the same sacrifices time and time again.
And it is all to no purpose. Those many sacrifices can never
take away sin. In any case you are now out of date. Those
sacrifices need no longer be offered. The Messiah has offered
himself, once for all, in a sacrifice to end all sacrifices. And
his sacrifice does take away sin. Repent and commit yourself
to Jesus in baptism. He will receive you and your life will
really begin. Take our word for it. We know the drudgery.
We know the ineffectiveness of it all. We have been through
it. And now we are free, living, joyous. Come and join us. All
that we tried to do as priests has been accomplished in him."

Doctors can talk to doctors in their own language. Lawyers
can enter discussion with lawyers because they share the
same legal interests and employ the same categories. So
priests could testify to priests and against their own background "preach to them Jesus"—even in a conversation.

We pass on to consider another group, those who arrested
Jesus. The high priests and their satellites had plotted to
arrest him by means of a trick and then to kill him. Judas
was part of the "trick," and Jesus was arrested. A whole
crowd came out to do it, unnecessarily armed with swords
and clubs. Did they think he was a brigand? They could have
taken him any day when he was sitting quietly in the Temple,
teaching. In fact they took him in the Garden of Gethsemane,
and detained him.

Let us now choose one of the crowd, one of the underlings
of the high priests and Pharisees, and bring him face to face
with the Philippian jailer (Acts 16:23–34). What could the
Christian jailer say to him?

We have something in common, he could say. You were
under orders and so was I. You were ordered to make an
arrest; I was ordered to guard arrested men and keep them
in security in my prison. But your background is different
from mine. You belong to the chosen nation. You have lived
from birth in an atmosphere of religion, of the service of the
one true God. You live in the holy city and under the shadow
of the Temple. You cannot fail to be constantly reminded of
the living God, of his awe-ful presence in Israel and of the

moral and spiritual demands he makes on men. And yet you let yourself be tricked into arresting the holiest Man that ever lived in Israel. This was in spite of a reminder given at the very time of the arrest. Do you remember how he answered when he was told that they were looking for Jesus of Nazareth? He used the language of Deity, "I am." Do you remember how they recoiled and fell to the ground? (John 18:6; cf. 7:46; 8:58). Yet you went on with the business. You thought that you were arresting and detaining him. So you were, in a sense. But he let himself be arrested. He could not long be detained. "It was not possible for him to be detained" by death itself (Acts 2:24).

Do you people fail to realize that you have the externals of religion but deny the reality? When you took the Lord to the governor's residence you would not go inside. You feared that on heathen ground you would be defiled and not be able to eat the Passover. Yet to be accomplices in a murder would not defile! (If he had known centuries in advance, the jailer could have told of the brigands in Eastern Europe who would cut your throat for your money but obstinately refuse to eat meat in Lent.)

The Lord was master of the situation, and he did not call a halt to what was going on. God did not intervene to stop it either. Jesus went to the cross—for the benefit of people like you and me.

My background is different from yours. I did not belong to the right company. There was little to remind me of God. I did not have even the externals of religion with its inner promise. I was on the point of suicide and I was stopped. Jesus went to his death and was not stopped, either by himself or by God. Can you suggest a reason to account for this? I will tell you. At least this is how it comes home to me. Jesus went to his death to open the door to God. I was restrained in order that by his death I might enter the door and come to God. I received mercy.

This mercy is for you too. You must have a good many sins on your conscience, as I had. If you have no conscience, you still have the sins. You can get rid of them. Suppose you do what I did—and I can recommend it. Come to the Lord—

for he is Lord and Savior—come to the Lord, Jesus Christ. You did this once before. Come to him now in a different way. You once came to arrest him. Come to him and say, "Lord, will you lay your hands on me and arrest me? Will you detain me? You are the only Savior and the only One for me."

At the time of the arrest of Jesus the disciples wondered if they should offer resistance. Without waiting for permission, Peter impulsively lunged forward with his sword and struck at the servant of the high priest, Malchus. He seems to have bungled it in his impetuosity—unless he were left-handed—because he cut off Malchus's *right* ear. It was hardly calculated to repel an invasion! Casualties: one ear— no heart-thrust, no head wound, no dead. At once the Lord healed and restored the ear (Luke 22:50–51; John 18:10–11), with a rebuke for Peter. What could Peter have said after Pentecost if he met Malchus?

We can at once dismiss as unworthy any lighthearted remarks such as: "How's the ear getting on, Malchus? No more trouble?" The situation is far too serious for that. Malchus must be won, not further antagonized. He might have brought trouble on Peter. At any rate only John's Gospel reveals the name of Peter as that of the attacker, when presumably at a later date it was safe to do so. In any case Peter had a higher motive than that of merely putting himself out of danger. He had learned to live with danger and his interest was in making the gospel known.

He might begin like this. I have been hoping to meet you, Malchus. There is something which needs to be put right. I am sorry I lost my head and struck you when they came to arrest the Lord. I put myself in the wrong badly. Will you forgive me? I can tell you this: the Lord himself has forgiven me for my folly, and for much worse. I boasted that I was ready to die for him and then I went and said I didn't know him.

You are an exceptional man, Malchus. Do you realize that you are the only person the Lord healed without being asked? Unless my memory is at fault, his acts of healing were always done in response to an appeal to him. He had wonderful hands, as you know well. He touched people with them, and they had a healing touch. He touched the eyes of the blind and they regained their sight. He touched a man's tongue and restored his power to speak. He once touched a funeral bier and stopped the procession—and raised the body to life again. The poor little widow was weeping for her only son and it moved him to pity. He even touched a leper and made him clean. And now you have joined the company. On one occasion he put his fingers into a man's ear, and the deaf man heard again. He did more than that for you: you were not deaf but had lost an ear. And at once he healed it.

If he treated you like that without being asked, what do you think he would do if you asked him? I can tell you, because of what he did for me. I said just now that he touched a leper. It was a dreadful thing to do—to touch that mass of impurity. Doesn't it show how much he loved people? But he did more. The leprosy was one man's impurity. Suppose that all the world were lepers and suppose that all the accumulated mass of uncleanness could be concentrated in one spot. We should all avoid it like the plague! But we are all moral and spiritual lepers. All our uncleanness, all our sins, have been brought together into one "spot." Where do you think they met?

They met, so to speak, on Jesus' back. He himself bore our sins in his body on the tree (1 Pet. 2:24). When you people arrested him, you thought that you had him in your hands and were going to do away with him. You thought that you—through the Romans, of course—would crucify him and get rid of him. As a matter of fact he had a date with destiny—which is a way of saying that it was God's will, gladly accepted by him. There on the cross he was to meet, and bear, all the sins that ever were or will be. Yours and mine, Malchus.

I spoke of what he did for me. He did just that. He bore my sins. And when he met me afterwards—yes, it is quite true; I spent forty days with him after God had raised him from the dead—he forgave me all my sins. Because, you see, he had already borne them. After his resurrection and his time with us, everything was made clear. He opened up the scriptures to us as a man will open up unexplored territory, putting in great main roads and linking up every part, so that all roads in scripture lead to—not Rome but—the cross. We then realized all that he had meant when he talked to us at the last supper before his passion. You won't understand that reference—not yet, anyway. But what about it, Malchus? Without being asked, he healed your ear. Would you like him to heal your heart? You might say that it did not cost him much to heal your ear. But what did it cost to heal your heart? to forgive your sins? to bear your sins? You must have some idea. I expect you saw him suffer. Confess your sins to him—as I did. Admit to him—he will hear!—that you are a sinner and that you trust him utterly. See what happens!

Can you please tell me how I can get in touch with your relation—your cousin or brother? He was in the garden with you and the others (John 18:26) and is one of the servants of the high priest. I rather want to see him.

So Peter comes in contact with the relation of Malchus. How could he begin? He would have to go back to that first unfortunate meeting.

Do you recall, he might ask, how you once asked me a question? You thought you recognized me and you were right. You are a servant of the high priest, I think? You were in the party that came to arrest Jesus. I blundered into an attack on your relation, Malchus, and cut off his ear. Jesus healed it at once—and put me in my place, too. Later, while Jesus was under examination, we were in the high priest's courtyard, warming ourselves round the fire. You recognized me and said, "Didn't I see you in the garden with him?"

Would you like to ask me that question again? You see, I told you that you had not seen me in the garden, and I told you a lie. And worse: I denied any knowledge of Jesus or any connection with him. As a matter of fact I had been a follower of his for some time. I had been closely with him— and I am still. So ask me again! And I will tell the truth. I was with him. I am with him. I hope that I shall ever be with him. He has forgiven me everything, all that I ever was or did, and he has put me to work for him in his service. I seek nothing better.

May I now turn the tables and ask you a question or two, not to embarrass you—as you once embarrassed me!—but rather to help? How do you like working for the high priest? Do you sometimes wonder if the mixture of religion and politics is good for everybody? especially the high priest's mixture? How can a religious man plot the death of an innocent man? Pilate saw no fault in him and what's more, he smelled a rat. He could see that it was not pure justice which delivered Jesus to the Romans. How do you think the high priest will feel on the next Day of Atonement when he confesses the sins of the people—and his own—and goes into the very presence of God in the Holy of Holies? Would you like to be in his shoes?

Now Jesus is alive: God raised him from the dead, and one day the high priest and all the rest of them—and you too—will stand before him. He is to judge the living and the dead. It is a terrifying thought: every day you live you get nearer to that judgment seat. Pilate's tribunal is child's play compared with his. You have been mixed up in this affair, to add to all your other sins. Would you like to be free of them? This same Jesus is Lord and Savior. In virtue of that cross—and you had a hand in it, didn't you?—God will pardon you if you commit yourself to Jesus. Then you too will be with him, not "in the garden" but all through life and at the Judgment Day itself. And he too will be with you.

We leave Simon Peter for another Simon, Simon the Zealot (Acts 1:13). His title suggests that at some time he had been a member of a movement whose watchword was "liberation." Such people did not endear themselves to the Roman occupying power! Simon had left behind all his political activities and had transferred his zeal to the service of our Lord. What could he say if he met a man who was still where Simon had been? He would certainly understand Barabbas. At the time of the Lord's crucifixion, Barabbas was in jail, a notorious prisoner, a rebel and a murderer

(Mark 15:7). He was a "freedom fighter," always on the run, whose ruthless use of force had become a second nature. He had been caught, but Pilate released him to the clamoring Jews instead of Jesus (Mark 15:15).

Simon might begin by asking if Barabbas was now "lying low" and seeking to escape the public eye. Had he given up his earlier hazardous life? How did you feel, Barabbas, when you walked out of the prison? You were due for crucifixion —and then released. Which thought struck you first—that you were free or that you were the hero of the hour?

You are living on borrowed time. You owe your life to someone else. He went to his cross and you did not. You gained the benefit. Did you feel grateful?

I might have been in your position but earlier on; and at that time there would have been no Jesus in captivity to take my place. But he delivered me nonetheless. He stopped me, laid hold of me, changed me. I have more than you, Barabbas, but you can have what I have.

At the moment you have a sort of amnesty. I have been given an absolute discharge: not guilty, innocent, justified. You were set free by the Roman governor, a weak and vacillating man who against his better judgment had to release you to a shouting mob. I was given my freedom by the King. You have heard of the kingdom of God? You were liberated to the crowd. What will they do to you? Will they hound you on to further violent follies which can only end in a cross after all? I was set free by the King and for the King's service. If you go back to the old life, you may have the thrill of adventure, the excitement of pitting your wits against superior powers, the momentary exultation when your dagger strikes home. I have joy unspeakable and full of glory, not the intermittent flush of triumph, but a deep and abiding satisfaction. Yours would be the temporary victory of a skirmish; I serve a King who is bound to win forever. Yours is secular; mine is heavenly. You, if you only realized it, are tearing the community to pieces; I am building it up. Your cause has no future: as the Lord said, those who take to the sword will perish with the sword. My cause is the cause of the One who died for your release and who died for my sins.

If—or rather when—you are caught again, there will be nobody to take your place on the cross. But the One who went to his cross for me and bore my sins—God raised him from the dead. He is with me still to bless. And more: you will have nobody to die for you, Barabbas; have you any one to speak to God for you? Murder is against God's commandment, as you know well, and he will judge you for it. Alone, and before the judgment seat of God: it's a poor future. But Jesus speaks for all his people and God listens to him.

All this can be yours. Drop this violent life, this unfeeling ruthlessness which in the end will bring no gain but eternal loss. Drop the desire to be a national hero, the darling of the populace, the great Barabbas. Come humbly to Jesus, Lord and Savior as he is. You will find that he died for you in another sense. He not only endured the nails and sword which were meant for you. He bore your guilt and sin—a heavy load!—that God might take you to his heart. I know this, for this is how he treated me. And he has given me a joyous zeal for him—a joy and a zeal I never knew as a freedom fighter.

Barabbas and Simon the Zealot steal away together, perhaps to a Christian meetingplace to meet believers in Jerusalem and to make arrangements for baptism. As they pass out of sight, a group of young men comes sauntering along, mingling with others on the street yet maintaining their cohesion as a party enjoying some leisure. As they walk, one nudges the other. "See that fellow over there? I can tell you something about him. When Jesus was being examined by the high priests and the council, they were trying to find some evidence against him so as to execute him, but they couldn't find anything. So some men stood up and committed perjury. They gave 'evidence' against him which was false. But it didn't work out as well as might have been hoped. Their stories didn't agree! That fellow was one of them. He is a liar" (Mark 14:55–59).

"Well, what about it?" says his companion. "What has it got to do with us?" "Don't you think we ought to go and give him a warning?" rejoins the first.

Why did he want to give a warning? It is because the young men in question were what we should call morticians and they had seen what happens to false witnesses. A man named Ananias and his wife Sapphira were still fresh in their memory.

They cross the street and the original speaker goes up to the "liar." The others stand round and leave the matter in his hands. He asks to be excused for the intervention, for he is a polite and tactful man, and then goes on. We think we ought to tell you, he says, that you are in great danger. We happen to know that you gave evidence at the examination of Jesus, and it came out that your evidence was not true. In fact you were telling lies. I know that God has raised Jesus from the dead, but it does not alter your position. You gave false evidence against him, knowing it was false. You are in danger.

The listener grows pale and looks as if he would try to run away. But by this time all the group has come up and they surround him. He thinks that they are about to attack him physically or that they want to do a deal with him—some form of blackmail. But this is not the case. He can only stand still and listen to what is said.

We are not threatening you. We just want to give you a warning. You are in danger. We have just seen what happens to false witnesses. A man came and offered money for God's work. He pretended that it was all he had, but in actual fact he had kept some back for himself. It was a terrible sin. He was dead and buried within three hours. Without knowing anything about it, his wife came in and told the same false story. She died too.

How do we know? We are morticians and the business came to us.

Do you realize that you were trying to help those whose one object was to bring about the death of God's Messiah? They did bring it about, but it was all within God's plan and he has raised him from the dead. We are his disciples. You are burdened with a heavy load of guilt, but God has spared you up to this moment. There is not a minute to lose. The One you tried to kill is the Savior and he is willing to save you. Confess this and all your sin to him, seek his pardon and trust him. He will receive you with love and mercy as his disciples, and you must come and join us. He is the truth and you must not tell any more lies (Acts 5:1–11). We are committed to the truth.

As we roam about Jerusalem we come across some unknown people who are still excitedly talking about somebody they met on the Day of Pentecost. Apparently there was a man called Simon (another one!) who hailed from Cyrene in North Africa, west of Egypt, who was coming into the city from the country when Jesus was being led out to his crucifixion. As he was passing by, he was "conscripted" to shoulder the Lord's cross and carry it for him (Mark 15:21). When the task was over he was dismissed and went about his business. Nearly two months later his attention was called to a large gathering of people. Somebody seemed to be holding an open-air meeting. He moved nearer to investigate.

Somebody was making a speech. He was somewhat at a loss, but the bystanders seemed friendly, and in the end he asked quietly, "What's it all about?" "Listen to the speaker," came the answer; "he's just named him. It's about Jesus of Nazareth." "Where have I heard that Name?" muttered Simon to himself (Acts 2:14–41).

Later on he saw another crowd and the same speaker. This time arrests were made (3:11–4:3). He was still rather puzzled until suddenly he remembered: the man whose cross he had carried all those weeks ago had been called Jesus.

He continued with his normal affairs until one day he ran into some of the group which had been near to him at the original meeting. They renewed acquaintance and talked of the great crowd and its impact. As the subject opened up, Simon told them of what he had now remembered. "That Jesus—he was crucified and I carried his cross for him." They all stared at him.

Then one of them burst out: "What a wonderful experience for you!" This took him aback. "Wonderful? It hurt. I was sore for days. Those Romans don't give you much time." But they all seemed very excited and crowded round him.

Simon! Don't you realize? The Jesus whose cross you carried is the Messiah. He had raised the hope that he was the promised Redeemer of Israel. Then he was crucified. His crucifixion shattered the hope. But God raised him from the dead. He is the Redeemer—and you helped him in his work.

At this point, before Simon could answer, another intervened. That is not very well put, though I know what you mean. Simon's help was like that of the Lord's mother. She gave him food when he was a baby. If she had not done so, he would have starved. She helped him by keeping him alive. Or think of those women who followed him. They were well off and supplied Jesus' needs after he had left his home and his work for his public ministry and had no income. They helped him in this way. But neither his mother nor the women helped him in his work of redemption. Simon did not help either. Simon carried the wood of the cross; Jesus bore our sins. Simon was compelled to carry the cross; Jesus did it of his own free will. Simon probably did not think of God's will coming into the picture, and he probably indulged in some cursing; Jesus went to the cross in obedience to God's will. Simon hated the whole business; Jesus did it for the joy which was set before him. Simon was inconvenienced; Jesus died. With all due respect to Simon, he was not indispensable: if he had not been available, those Romans would have found somebody else. But there is only one Jesus. There is no other Savior; nobody apart from him.

Simon had been listening in silence. Now he said, rather awkwardly, and with hesitation: I never thought of that. What do you think I ought to do? The answer came in a flash. You can get something out of this, just as we did. You did? What did you get out of it?

They almost tumbled over one another in their eagerness to speak. We repented of our sins and we turned right round away from them and came to Jesus. Yes! He is alive. He received us and all our sins have been blotted out. To show that we really meant it all, we were baptized. We received the Holy Spirit and life, real life, then began. If you want to check up on us, there are hundreds and thousands in this city, just like us. They live, because of Jesus. They live, for him. Come and join us.

Around the cross of Jesus were some rough and hard-bitten men. Bloodshed did not worry them, for they were used to it. The pain of others left them quite unmoved. "Sitting down they watched him there." But there was one man present who has been called "the compassionate soldier." He ran and filled a sponge with cheap wine, fixed it to a cane and offered it to the Crucified. The wine could be sucked from the sponge. A cup would have been useless. It was a thoughtful, kindly act, perhaps impulsive—or why did he run?

Let us suppose that this man in the course of his duties fell in with Cornelius, the converted Roman centurion (Acts 10:1-2, 44), and spent some time with him. They indulge in reminiscences. Perhaps Cornelius "steered" the conversation. At any rate they come round to the Name of Jesus and the soldier tells his new acquaintance all about the crucifixion. In the detailed story he mentions the incident of the sponge. This gives Cornelius his opportunity.

That was a very kind act on your part, he says; pretty well exceptional, I should think. We are a rough race of men and do not often give time and thought to deeds like that. It does you credit. But even so I have found that kindness is not enough. I used to do that sort of thing—I hope I still do. I had a soft spot for many people. I used to be what they called a "God-fearer." I got attached to the Jewish synagogue because there were points about these people which I found admirable. They believe in one God, and in one God only. They have no images in their worship, as God is invisible. Their code of morals is high. I was not exactly "one of them," but they made me welcome and I was "one with them." I found their worship helpful, prayed to their God and tried to obey his commandments, and went in for quite a lot of almsgiving. Some people are in great trouble, poor things. In all these activities my family was quite content to come along with me.

No doubt I was like you—exceptional. Not many centurions are to be found in the synagogue! But it was not enough. It is a long story and I will stick to the main points. In rather amazing circumstances, "a man with a mission" came and told me about Jesus—the Man you helped with the sponge. He died on the cross, as you well know, but God raised him from the dead. He is going to be the Judge of everybody when the time comes, but in the meantime something marvelous is available. Through him—the coming Judge!—anyone who believes in him can get the forgiveness of his sins. For he is what the Jewish people call the Messiah, the Deliverer whom God promised to send. Anyone! I am not a Jew, but even so I am not ruled out on that account. In fact, God sent his man to tell me all about it, and my family as well. We were eligible for salvation, if we did what God said—believe in Jesus. I had many kindnesses to my credit, as I am sure you have, but our kindnesses will not help us when we meet Jesus as our Judge. I have already met him as the Savior, and he has received me and forgiven all my sins. When I finally meet him as Judge, he will prove to be Savior still. There are many people who have traveled the same road as I have, both Jews and others, and we are a wonderful fellowship. Jesus the Christ, Lord and Savior, is always with us. We meet together to worship God through him. I wish more of the Jews would come, because Jesus fulfills all their hopes. But some of them refuse to believe and insist on going on with their services in the synagogue—without Jesus and without salvation, alas!

What about you?

We leave Cornelius as he is about to come to close quarters with his acquaintance and meet another soldier. We call him the man with the hammer and nails. There may have been more than one, as three were crucified—two men later known as the penitent and the impenitent thief, and Jesus (Luke 23:33–43). There must have been at least one who drove the nails into the Lord (John 19:23–24). He did not shrink from the task. Living flesh and sensitive nerve meant nothing to him. When he had finished his task he calmly took his share of the Lord's clothes and equally calmly agreed not to split up the seamless tunic but to toss up for it. He was cold-blooded to the marrow.

But he had forgotten—or had not been informed—that Jesus was known as the Carpenter of Nazareth. The matter is brought up when his path crossed that of the apostle Paul. It may be that Paul spoke of Christ crucified, and that the soldier, who had since heard about the Christian movement, repelled his advance with mockery. Christ? You mean Jesus? Oh yes, I remember; you said, "crucified," didn't you? I drove the nails into him.

Did you? said Paul. You have omitted a most important part of the story. He was a carpenter, you know, and most skilled at his work. When you drove in the nails you thought you had him at your mercy. Well, you were wrong. He was driving in nails, too. Let me explain.

If your commanding officer, or come to that, Caesar himself, had strictly laid it down that there were to be no more crucifixions, you would be in trouble, I think. Disobedience to orders! There would be a court-martial with you in the dock and the charge would be read out. The document could have very serious consequences for you. Now we have all been disobedient to orders, God's orders, and he brings a charge against us. We are all in trouble.

But while you were hammering in your nails, the Carpenter was hammering in his. He took the written accusation and nailed it to his cross (Col. 2:14). All our sins—and cruelties —he saw summed up in handwriting. They were very clear; and he took them all upon himself. That leaves us clear.

Now, soldier, you have been in trouble. Here is a way out, with a new Commander-in-Chief as well, to love and bless you. . . .

St. Paul goes on to explain the way of salvation and we ourselves go on to bring two centurions together. We have met one of them before, Cornelius, and shall not linger. We shall rather leave Cornelius to remind his fellow centurion of what he said when Jesus died. He seems to have been very emphatic. "Truly this man was the Son of God" (Matt.

27:54; Mark 15:39, KJV); "in reality this was a righteous man" (Luke 23:47). Some people may think that "Son of God" on the lips of a heathen Roman does not mean all that a Christian believer knows to be in the term. That is just our point. And we leave Cornelius to expound the deeper meaning. He might begin by saying that "was" is not the end of the story. . . .

It would be instructive to introduce the soldier who pierced the side of Jesus (John 19:34) to the man who heard this same Jesus say, from heaven, "Saul, Saul, why are you persecuting me?" (Acts 9:4). I wonder how the conversation would go between two governors, Sergius Paulus of Cyprus, a shrewd man who became a Christian (Acts 13:7, 12), and Pontius Pilate of Judea, who asked, "What is truth?" (John 18:38) and stayed not for an answer? It might lead to exciting results if a conference could be arranged between the many Jews who read the inscription on the cross, "Jesus of Nazareth the King of the Jews" (John 19:19–22) and the Samaritans who "believed Philip when he told the good news about the kingdom of God and the Name of Jesus Christ" (Acts 8:12). But what should we hear if we were told the tale of the two servant girls?

In an early stage of the Passion, our Lord was brought to the house of the high priest, and Peter and another disciple were following. The other disciple had the entrée and went with Jesus into the courtyard, leaving Peter outside. He shortly returned, had a word with the girl on duty at the door, and then took Peter with him into the courtyard. There can be little doubt that what he said to the girl cleared the way for Peter to enter. There for a moment we can leave them (John 18:15–17).

Now there is another maidservant, Rhoda, whom we now introduce to the high priest's servant. We shall observe them as they talk together and shall listen especially to Rhoda. She will probably have something very interesting to say (Acts 12:13–17). After a preliminary conversation in which they are trying to "get acquainted," Rhoda takes the lead.

I think we have something in common. You are a maid in the service of the high priest. You were on duty the night they brought in Jesus for examination, and one of his disciples had no difficulty in getting into the courtyard. But he left his friend, Peter, outside. After a time he came back and reassured you, and in consequence you admitted Peter as well. I once had to admit Peter in rather different circumstances, but at any rate we have this in common: we both let him in. But now our paths diverge.

When Peter came in you spoke to him in some surprise. "What? Not another one? You're not one of the disciples of this Man, are you?" You had admitted him because he had been vouched for by somebody else, and when you asked him a question you virtually put the answer into his mouth. You said, "You're not . . . are you?" and you almost made him say "no." That started him downwards and he was not able to pull himself up. It was a cold night and Peter was glad to join the other men round the fire in the yard. At first they just accepted him, saying almost exactly what you had said. *"You*'re not one of his disciples, are you?" Then in the light of the fire one of the men recognized him. They had both been in the garden when Jesus was arrested, and Peter had drawn attention to himself. He had used his sword! The truth must surely come out now. But Peter still denied it (John 18:25–27).

So much for what we have in common. It was once my business to answer the door. Peter was in prison and we were holding a prayer meeting at our house. We were earnestly praying for him. Suddenly there was a bang at the door. I slipped quietly out of the meeting to see who was there, and when I got to the door I said, "Who is it?" before opening up. You can't be too careful these days. When he answered I recognized Peter's voice.

I was so bowled over that I forgot to open the door! I did a dreadful thing. I burst right into the meeting as they were praying. "Peter's at the door!" They told me—they had stopped praying—that I was crazy and I had to insist, telling them again and again that it was true. All the time Peter was banging away and trying to get in—like answers to some of our prayers!—and in the end they suddenly changed their minds and tried to do my job for me, rushing in a crowd to the door. In he came. He waved us into silence and then told

us a marvelous tale of how the Lord—the One he had denied!
—had brought him out of prison to escape for a time to us.

You let him in, rather reluctantly perhaps, and then you
tripped him up. I kept him out, for sheer joy; and then
joined the others and let him in. And we all listened to him.

He was a different man. You met him when he was a
coward. When I let him in he was not afraid of anybody,
even the rulers—including your employer, the high priest—
even when they threatened him (Acts 4:5–6, 17–21). He had
addressed great crowds of people—ever tried to make a
speech?—and he did not flatter them, either. He accused
them, informed them, guided them, got himself arrested,
escaped and then took to the offensive by teaching the people
in the Temple. He was flogged but it did not stop him (Acts
5:25, 40–42).

How do you explain the change? He now "denied himself"
(3:12) and told the crowds all about the One whom he had
denied. The people had repudiated Jesus too, even when
Pilate had made the judicial decision to release him. But
Jesus was—and is—the Messiah, and God raised him from
the dead. Peter had forty days with him after his resurrection, and Jesus forgave him everything. The resurrection of
Jesus made all the difference to—and in—Peter (1 Pet. 1:3).
Jesus is now seated in authority at the right hand of God
and he has sent the Holy Spirit to be with his people. It is
through the power of the Holy Spirit that Peter makes his
speeches and convinces people so that they begin to believe
in Jesus after all. When they do this he forgives them all
their sins.

Now I am going to tell you a secret. It's not a secret really
and I don't mind who knows. But it's like a secret in being
like the thoughts which you think. Nobody knows what you
are thinking until you tell them. It's something that goes on
"inside." Perhaps I can put it in a way which will help you
to understand. Do you remember your work as a maid? You
had to open the door to let people come in. You were—and
perhaps still are—a doorkeeper. I am a doorkeeper too—in
more senses than one.

When Peter preaches the gospel of Jesus, the risen Messiah, he tells them all that Jesus has done for them—he died for their sins. Peter then says that they must repent—leave their sins behind them forever—and turn to Jesus. When they have thus come to him, they must trust him. Like a doorkeeper, they must open the door to him, the door of their heart. I did just that. I opened the door of my heart and Jesus the Messiah, Savior and Lord, came in. Will you open the door?

We are nearing the end of our taste of the Acts of the Apostles. Before we pass on to the Epistles we might attempt a summary. The Word has been looming larger, the numbers of Christians are increasing, the church is growing, the geographical area is widening, a simple ministerial organization is developing, and the cleavage between believer and unbeliever is seen to be sharper and deeper. From the first beginnings in Jerusalem to the apostle Paul's arrival in Rome, we can watch a process—the emergence of what is generally called *Christianity*. What is Christianity?

First of all, it is a fact. It is an event. It is more than a system of ideas, however true. It is a fact, a complex fact made up of a number of facts. They can be stated as truths and arranged cohesively as a system, but the system would be nothing without the antecedent fact. It is something that happened.

But we must not stand back and merely observe it, wonderful as it is. Each believing man—and only the believer can finally judge, because he sees it from the inside—knows that in addition to fact or event, it is experience. It starts—as experience—when the Word is heard, whether read or preached or just brought into conversation. A man says, I heard it. This is experience. He is not a block of wood or a tape recorder. He is what is called an experient subject. *He,* or his "ego," hears. When he hears, he believes: believes the facts as stated and trusts the Person who is the subject of the statements. *He* believes. *He* receives Christ, *he* is illuminated, *he* is born again, *he* knows himself to have become a child of God, *he* is now possessed of the Holy Spirit. Each believer can say: Christianity is something that happened;

134 WORD SURVEY OF THE NEW TESTAMENT

and secondly, and on the basis of the fact, it is something
that happened to me.

But he is not alone and he is not left alone. He is not the
only man in the world; and he is not the only believer in the
world. Others have believed before him; others believe at
the same time as he does; others will go on believing in the
future. There is a chorus of voices, some sounding high notes
and others low, some singing slowly and some quickly; but
all are saying the same: in the words of Isaac Watts's hymn
"Give me the wings of faith," they

> Ascribe their conquest to the Lamb,
> Their triumph to His death.

Each and all converge on Christ; each and all belong to
Christ; and therefore they all belong to one another. Deep
answers to deep, for they all enjoy a common life. In any case
the new convert has a public initiation into the fellowship.
The church has been commanded by the Lord to baptize and
the convert has been commanded to submit to baptism.
Christianity is thus a fact, an experience and a fellowship. It
is something which happened to *us*.

It is also a task as well as an enjoyment, a discipline as
well as a consolation. Christianity has a program which it
is the duty of all believers in the fellowship to carry out.
First comes duty to God. He is to be worshiped, in private
and in public, alone and with others. Within the area of
worship, prayer is to be maintained and the scriptures read
and heard. The sacraments are to be administered regularly
and the Word is to be preached and taught. Then comes duty
to man—which is also commanded by God. The moral law
is to be obeyed and "good works" done. In a word, discipleship is more than a name. Christianity is something which
ought to happen.

Fifthly and finally, Christianity is a hope. "This Jesus who
was taken up from you into heaven will thus come in the
manner in which you gazed upon him as he went into heaven"
(Acts 1:11). It is not a vague thought that "something some
day will happen." It is a strong expectation of the Lord's
personal appearance in power and majesty. It is not based

on reason, though reason may support the thought. It is based on revelation. The fixing of dates and the making of calculations are ruled out: "it is not yours to know times or seasons which the Father put in his own authority" (Acts 1:7). Christianity is assuredly something that will happen.

The fact of Christ; the personal experience of knowing him; the warmth of fellowship; the challenge of duty to God and to man; the certainty of the hope: these have emerged in the Acts of the Apostles as a convenient summary of the faith, the essence of Christianity.

5.

The Epistles:
The Apostles Elaborating
and Applying the Gospel

THE EPISTLES RESEMBLE those parts of the Acts in which we
are given a record of an address by a Christian to Christians.
As a rule the Epistles are much longer, and of course they
are written and not spoken. At times in the Epistles we may
hear an echo of the spoken word, perhaps even a conscious
or unconscious quotation from a speech. But it is incorporated into the letter, which remains a letter and not an
anthology. As we savor the Epistles, we shall begin with a
taste of that which was written "to the Romans."

The Epistle to the Romans

It has sometimes been asked whether Romans is a letter
or a treatise. The development of its theme and the density
and profundity of its thought may on occasion bring us down
on the side of the treatise. But the form is that of a letter,
not only in its beginning and ending but in its personal details and its general warmth and feeling. It may well be that
Paul has "incorporated" some of his preaching material into
his letter, but we must not think of his frenzied search for
some sermon notes in order to get his quotation (of himself!)
correct. It flowed out from his mind naturally and easily as
he wrote or dictated, just as a pastor in writing on a weighty
subject to his congregation might find himself—when he
read it over—putting into written form phrases and sentences which he had used, perhaps many times, in sermons.

He is not "quoting" in the usually accepted sense. He thinks
like this, he talks like this and so he writes like this. Paul the
Christian believer, Paul the theologian, Paul the evangelist,
Paul the pastor, was one and the same man, and as we read
the letter we see him in one aspect or another or in a combination of two or more aspects; but it is the same man and
he is still writing a letter. Given the amount of space which
he took and the subject with which he desired to deal, it
was perhaps inevitable that some should see his product as
a treatise. But it is not "theoretical." It is a letter.

Paul was writing to a church which he had not founded
and had not even visited. He had long been hoping and praying that it would be within the divine will for him to come
to the Roman Christians. In the meantime he wanted them to
know what it was that he really preached. They may have
heard distorted rumors about him. Now they could have the
truth from its source. The result is a classical exposition of
the gospel. It is theoretical or formal in the sense that it can
be applied to all sorts and conditions of men. It is not composed for a readership of the same stamp. It is not "the
gospel for philosophers—Christ the wisdom of God." It is
not "the gospel for slaves—Christ the Liberator." It is not
"the gospel for magistrates—Christ the Lord of heaven and
earth." It is not "the gospel for seekers—Christ the Desire
of all nations." It is just—the gospel: Christ the Savior of
sinners. There were plenty of all types, in Rome and elsewhere, and the gospel, formulated in "general" terms, can be
applied to any and every particular man, woman, and child,
in Rome or anywhere else. Hence, it has been said, Romans
has been at the heart of every revival.

St. Paul took seven verses to say what we should say in
less than seven words. In business we begin with "Dear Sir."
In church circles we should observe the warm courtesies by
saying "Dear Friend" or perhaps "Dear Brother." If we
were writing to a senior citizen who was highly and widely
respected, we should start off with "Dear Mr. X." With Paul
it all streamed forth like the waters of Niagara or a torrential
river. In a sense what was within him had to come out and
it burst forth. But it did not "merely" burst forth. Or if it

did, it was a bursting forth of thought as well as feeling. It revealed the warmth of the preacher rather than the coolness of the essayist, but it was the warmth of a preacher who was also a thinker. His words and phrases have implications for the readers.

He begins: "Paul, a slave of Christ Jesus." He implies that he is not his own man. He has been bought with a price. He has a new Owner. He is under orders. If there is any starch in the church of Rome and any are disposed to wonder who this man is who presumes to write to them, he has already answered their questions. What business is it of his? He is under orders. There is nothing more to be said on that subject. He continues to write.

He is "an apostle by vocation." He has not satisfied an ambition, reached a pinnacle or appointed himself. He was called. If necessary he can tell them all about the Road to Damascus. They may have heard part of the story already. It was the Lord who had called him and appointed him an apostle. As an apostle, he had been "separated"—not for politics, not for the army, not for education, but for the gospel. Is there anything higher? It is God's gospel and the readers have already received it. He is surely right in counting on their sympathy for him and his work.

They must not imagine that his gospel is any different from theirs. He may be able to lead them into its deeper truths or indicate some aspects which they had forgotten or never learned. But it was and is the one gospel. It was not his invention and was nothing new. It had been promised by God long ago, and they can check up on him if they want to do so. It is all there, written down in permanent form in the scriptures. God had made his promise known through his prophets. If they want to check what the apostle says when he preaches and writes, let them read their Bibles!

The center of the gospel is to be found at one point, God's Son. Men saw him as a man, born of David's line, descended from the ancient king of Israel. Though his manhood was as clear as daylight, his deity was shrouded in a mist. But the mist was wafted away and he emerged into clear outline as the Son of God when he was raised from the dead. All power is his. He is Jesus Christ our Lord—our Lord, yours and mine. We enjoy the same redemption. We, you and I, take our orders from the same Authority. We are in the same camp.

This having been established, the apostle "comes closer" to his readers. Without making an argument of it or resorting to flattery, he combines personal experience and theological orthodoxy with appreciation of the stature of the Roman church. "I thank my God through Jesus Christ for you all, because your faith is talked of in all the world." He never omits them from his prayers. At long last somehow he will reach them, if it is God's will to answer his prayers. For he is yearning to see them. He plans to share with them some spiritual gift for their strengthening—that is (note the tact), to receive encouragement in their company through the interplay of their common faith.

He maintains the "soft" approach. He does not say, "note this" or "enter this in the minute book." "I do not want you to be unaware, my brothers," that time and time again he had purposed to come to them but every time, right up to the present moment, he had been prevented. He wanted to work effectively among them as he had done everywhere else. He was under obligation to men of every type (Jesus the Lord had imposed the obligation), and hence was eager to preach the gospel to his readers also. You can preach the gospel to Christians. Paul is not ashamed of the gospel. It is the divine, saving and universal power. It bears no human imperfection, has no problems which would mar the salvation which it offers, and is not restricted to any particular group—only to those who believe. In it is revealed the righteousness of God.

It should be noticed how Paul has begun with the personal approach of a letter, has touched on Christian doctrine and truth and his own personal experience, has shown his appreciation of his readers and the compulsion within his own heart. This has brought him to the gospel and in it the righteousness of God. This is his "cue." He is able to make a natural transition to his theme, and he here begins the first main section of his letter.

Paul lays the foundation for his exposition by asserting
the sinfulness of men, a universal sinfulness. The picture
which he draws is frightening: he might be describing our
modern scene. If anyone doubts this, he should work through
the list of sins (1:29-32). Are any of them missing today?
They all spring from a wrong beginning, the suppression of
God's truth. Its consequence is idolatry. The men of today
need not smile at their superiority to such an outmoded activity. They should rather ask themselves the questions:
Whom, or what, do I worship? From whom do I take my
orders? It will not help anyone if he says that he takes his
orders only from himself.

The human heart is unintelligent, darkened, reduced to
futility even when it attempts to reason. In conduct it is
defiant. It persists in its evil course even when it knows its
final outcome, the punishment of death. Such an individual
is not in any sense an exception. Public opinion is on his
side.

Some have sought to modify Paul's view of the world of
his day. Was it as bad as he has pictured? Was there not
another side, a good and wholesome element? There was
indeed the presence of the elect of God. There were some
men of principle, of humanitarian sympathy, gifted in friendship, pure in family life, possessed of civic virtue and rising
far above a vulgar animality. But Paul has given us a
preacher's and prophetic insight into the state of a whole
civilization. It had its fairer side. So has the rosy apple, shiny
and inviting—but rotten at the core. The scene has been
described as the observable situation of the wrath of God.
Again we tremble: do we see the same wrath of God today?

The apostle omits nobody. Not a single righteous man can
be found. All are shut up in the prison house, "under sin."
All are answerable to God and all are without an answer to
give him. Jew and Gentile are alike and united in this if in
nothing else. The prospect is even darker than their own
minds.

"But now"—with a sigh of relief—he turns to his next
main section, the gospel which gives the answer. In Christ
the believer finds liberation from wrath, death, the law, sin.

He introduces his exposition with as tightly packed a statement as can be found in the whole of theological literature. Six verses (3:21–26) have the weight of volumes because of their density. It is not surprising that at Troas Paul could preach all night: he needed the time (Acts 20:7, 11).

A shallow cynicism has remarked that Paul's preaching was all too much for Eutychus: he fell asleep. He fell from the window ledge of the third story and lost his life, which the apostle magnanimously restored—and then went on preaching, from midnight till dawn. Again: Paul needed the time. Not so very long afterwards the elders of the church of Ephesus bade him farewell at Miletus. In Ephesus, for three years throughout night and day the apostle had not ceased to speak. A long session! Yet when the separation finally came, these same elders in an atmosphere of prayer burst forth in weeping and lamentation and kissed him tenderly, grieved above all that they would never see him again. Which shows the truer appreciation of Paul? Which has the appetite for the Word of God? Which is the keener to take every opportunity? The cynical mockery or the tears? (Acts 20:31, 36–38.)

Paul takes five chapters (4–8) to elaborate these six significant verses. He ends with the rhetorical question, "Who will separate us from the love of Christ?" and ransacks the whole universe for powers which would try. Adversity of any and every kind, life and death, present and future, scientific principles and supernatural beings, the vast sweep of time and space, everything in existence apart from God himself, all leave us super-conquerors through him who loved us. Nothing in creation will be able to separate us from (note the addition) the love of God which is in Christ Jesus our Lord. This is the logical climax of the earlier statement that God demonstrates his own love to us in the fact that while we were still sinners Christ died for us (5:8). It is an example of the certainty possessed by the believing man: through the gift of the Holy Spirit the love of God penetrates and permeates all the deep recesses of the heart (5:5).

Paul has cleared the way to the question, "Who will separate us. . . ?" by a series of questions in animated, declamatory, dramatic style. If there is to be any separation, it will start on our side, not on the divine side. The attack will be on us. We see therefore a succession of enemies, doing their worst against us with a developing inventiveness. Who is against us? Who of any significance could be, if God is for us? In sparing not his own Son, God includes everything in such a gracious gift. The insignificant are not convinced and look around for some means to press their attack. Ah! an accusation! They will bring a charge against them. They will drag them into court. What silliness is this? They are dealing with the elect of God. There can be no fear of the verdict, no doubt, no question. The accusers make a belated discovery. The One who justifies the elect is—God. Baffled, they retire in fury to seek some other plan. At last they have it. They set up their own court. They bribe the witnesses. They brief the judge. But who is he who will condemn? His verdict will never be implemented. It will never even be given. He will not be allowed to go so far. A new Figure appears on the scene. Christ Jesus is his Name. He is the One who died, unspared; more than that, was raised and is at the right hand of God in authority. He intercedes with God—for us. What does he say?

This court has not any authority whatsoever. It is a sinful invention, trespassing on the divine right. It arrogantly takes too much upon itself. It is no judge. In any case the verdict has been given. The condemnation has already fallen—on me. The "defendants" are under the protection of the divine court. Their debt has been paid. Father: stop the proceedings; dismiss the "court." Intervene—"for us." I was sent to die for them, and I did so die. I intercede for them—in accordance with thy will. It was for love of them that thou didst send me. Thou dost love them still. . . . Therefore

Who will separate us. . . ?

Three chapters follow (9–11) which are often called a digression. They deal with the history and destiny of Israel, in consequence of her rejection of the Messiah. But they are not entirely a digression. Something had to be said to explain why the prepared and privileged people of God should refuse to believe. Such a statement might help to temper any "superiority" of Jew or Gentile toward each other in the church. The "remnant" of Israel which did indeed believe is a hopeful sign that Israel will one day corporately return to the Lord. Her rejection has brought blessing to the Gentiles; what will her acceptance bring?

Paul now resumes the thought which was developed in the first eight chapters of Romans. Given these great facts of the gospel, what then? He "therefore" (12:1) urges his readers to consider their full Christian responsibility. Truth or doctrine is to be believed—and carried out in the life of discipleship. The apostle therefore gives detailed directions for Christian life. He touches on secular matters in the Christian doctrine of the civil state (13:1–7) and shows that the kingdom of God is not the "welfare state" raised to the highest degree. It is "not eating and drinking but righteousness and peace and joy in the Holy Spirit" (14:17).

The last or "farewell" chapter contains much of what today we should write as "give my love to. . . ." Here we see the very human side of this great Christian. For example, he sends greetings "to Rufus . . . and his mother and mine" (16:13). Paul's mother? It seems hardly likely. We have rather a clue to what journalists call a "human interest story." Rufus may well be the son of Simon of Cyrene, the compulsory cross-bearer for Jesus, mentioned in Mark 15:21. The mother of Rufus was one of the "mothers" given to those who had left home and family, including mother, for the sake of Jesus and the gospel (Mark 10:29–30). In some circumstances she had "mothered" him.

This is not as preposterous as it sounds. There comes a time when the woman's touch is needed. At Lystra Paul had been mobbed, stoned and dragged outside the city apparently dead. He arose and returned to the city, the next day starting off for Derbe (Acts 14:19–20). There is half a miracle in those intervening hours. Is it quite impossible that some motherly soul in Lystra brushed aside the men folk, wiped away the sweat and blood, applied poultices, "tempted" him with some appetizing dish and put him on his feet again? It would seem that Paul remembered such kindnesses. It is said that the sailor has a girl in every port. Perhaps the apostle had a mother in every mission station. It would be a fulfillment of the Lord's promise. Those who have abandoned all for him and for the gospel have mothers in plenty. Church life has wonderful compensations for those who are deeply in the fellowship—homes, brothers and sisters, mothers and children, and even property to enjoy—without the responsibility of maintenance!

It is not being said that the mother of Rufus was actually at Lystra. We have seen a typical example of what a mother might have done. If one "mother" acted thus at Lystra, the mother of Rufus could have done so somewhere else. At any rate Paul seems to make this suggestion.

The Epistles to the Corinthians

The apostle had an extensive correspondence. He wrote to Rome, which he had not visited, and he wrote to churches which he himself had founded. He had vivid memories of a year and a half in Corinth, and he had to keep in touch with the church there, as we see from the First and Second Epistles to the Corinthians. He could not forget Aquila and Priscilla, who had opened their home to him in Corinth (Acts 18:1-3). Paul wrote to the church because of information received, problems raised by and in the church, questions of doctrine, behavior and discipline, and painful personal matters. We cannot attempt an analysis of the letters but shall "taste" what is offered in them.

A great variety of matters comes before us as we read the First Epistle. Dangerous splits had occurred in the church (1:10-17). Parties had been formed, with an absent leader as their ideal. Some favored Paul the salvationist, others Apollos the intellectual; some looked to Cephas (we know him better as Peter) the ecclesiastic, and some, professing to be more spiritually minded, to Christ. Paul repudiates it all indignantly. The church should not be split. "Is Christ in pieces?" He turns to himself: "Paul was not crucified for you, was he?" They are setting their sights far too low. "What is Apollos? What is Paul?" They are only "servants through whom you gained your faith," no more. "I planted, Apollos watered, but God gave the increase" (3:5–6). Aim higher! You possess more than mere men. You have far more to be proud of. "Everything that exists is yours: Paul, Apollos, Cephas; the world itself; life and death, the present and the future; it's all yours, and you are Christ's and Christ is God's" (3:21–23). Christ guarantees your title to it, and God guarantees Christ. Enough of splits and sectional interests. Take it all!

There has been a lot of highfalutin talk about wisdom. They have not got to first base. They are immature, not yet ready for the Christian wisdom. They are babies in need of milk, not spiritual adults requiring meat. And the wisdom of this world is a dead-end street. The world through its philosophy did not know God. Christ is the wisdom of God. Forget the world's wisdom, learn Christ—and find in him the deep things of God (1:18–25; 2:6; 3:1–2).

Sex was a perennial problem at Corinth. The church had the loose Gentile world as its background. It had come from that style of life and had much to learn about individual purity and Christian marriage. A particularly nasty case of illicit sex required discipline, and the question of "spiritual marriage" had to be handled (5:1–13; 6:12–7:40).

Lawsuits between Christians excited the apostle's horror (6:1–11). It is not always easy for some of us to enter into his feelings. With centuries of Christian civilization behind us and often with Christian judges on the bench, we can understand men who seek a definite ruling of the court or who seek redress for some grievance by legal and official action rather than by "taking the law into their own hands." It is the law which is administered from the bench. If the law has received centuries of Christian inspiration and if the integrity and incorruptibility of the court is assured, that is one thing. Though a generation or two ago a lawsuit involving a main Christian denomination raised some eyebrows. But where the judges are just plain heathen, unsaved, unjustified, unjust (in the sense of unrighteous before God), it is at least anomalous for the saved, the justified, the just, to

seek justice from them. The just before the unjust: it is odd
for those who have received the benefit of Christ who died,
"the just for the unjust," to appear in court as adversaries
before those who are still unjust (1 Pet. 3:18), especially as
both parties have in Christ been brought to God. Is there
not even one solitary wise man in the church who could
settle the differences between Christian brethren? If there
is not, why don't they just let themselves be wronged?

The Corinthian background is different from our background today. Even so, Paul's attitude is a wise caution for
Christians. And the day might come when his words would
have to be applied more rigidly.

Paul warns his readers that the unjust will not inherit
the kingdom of God. Are they unaware of this? He adds a
long list of notorious sinners, fornicators, idolators, adul-
terers, homosexuals, thieves, drunks and the rest, who will
not inherit the kingdom of God. It is a desperate picture,
with dark and threatening clouds. Then the sun breaks
through. "And such were some of you; but. . . ." All salvation is contained in this "but." "Such were some of you; but
you were washed; but [he almost uses a finger to point the
contrast] you were sanctified; but you were justified in the
Name of the Lord Jesus Christ and in the Spirit of our God."
What a salvation! Even the judges can be saved; the experience of the Corinthian church proves it.

One of the problems at Corinth with which Paul had to
deal was the question of meat sacrificed to idols. It is hardly
a live issue for us today, but it brought real distress in
Corinth. Suppose the flesh of animals sacrificed to idols
finds its way into the butchers' shops. You buy it, cook it,
eat it: how does it differ from "ordinary" meat? The Christian with "knowledge" can take it all in his stride. Idols?
Nonsense! Blocks of wood and marble! There is but one
God. Eat it and enjoy it.

So far so good: such a man has knowledge. But though
the knowledge is necessary, a wrong use of it can be bad,
especially if it is used without love (1 Cor. 8:1, 7). That is
why the apostle says that "knowledge puffs up but love
builds." There is a solidity about love's productions. Knowl-

edge merely blows up a balloon. Knowledge "inflates"—in these days we ought to be able to understand the dangers. When does it thus inflate? It inflates, and its resulting "balloon" cannot be used for building purposes, when it leads its possessor to bully the man without it.

For here is a man who has faith but it is a weak faith. He has been converted to Christ out of heathenism but has not yet grasped with full conviction that there is but one God, the Lord of heaven and earth. For him the spell of the old gods has not been completely broken. He shudders at the thought of eating meat which had been sacrificed to them: what fate will befall him? For his former familiarity with idols is not dead. He senses a danger. And now a fellow Christian—with knowledge—starts to bully a man without knowledge. Eat it up! He does eat, and falls under the old spell. His weak conscience is defiled. He loses touch with Christ. A pitfall has become a downfall. It all happens because a Christian who can eat with safety has forced a Christian who cannot eat with safety. Knowledge has driven ignorance into a corner and the consequence is downfall.

Where has Christian love come in? The man with knowledge has forgotten the responsibility of knowledge, has forgotten that as a strong man he is his brother's keeper, the guardian of his weaker brother. This will not do. Better be a vegetarian than ruin your brother. Better be narrow-minded than lead your brother into the broad way which leads to destruction.

We are dealing with a historical situation which we are tempted to think is interesting but has no message for us. But it has a message for us, if we can only "translate" it.

It raises the whole question of what might be called "goods of questionable origin." We have seen today a revival of witchcraft. Supposing a witch or someone in her inner circle is converted to Christ. And suppose the local witch has a local business, making and selling meat pies and other eatables for a living. Suppose her trade is good, for she is an excellent cook. Even Christians delight in her pies. The new convert is troubled. The pies are not poisoned—scientific tests would prove the point. But are they in some way bewitched?

Local Christians enjoy the pies—"there's nothing wrong with them!"—and put pressure on the convert. Her faith is weak, her fears are irrational—and down she falls. And it was all because fellow Christians with knowledge insisted on their pies and were evangelists for them. Knowledge minus love can be a menace to the ignorant.

Or perhaps there is some factory or store nearby, and its excellent products are bought in great quantities by the church, perhaps even on a contractual basis. But it is known to everybody in town that the place is a sink of iniquity. Business is business: what is wrong in buying what is good from men who are evil?

But one of their workmen was converted recently, left his job in disgust and found other employment. After settling in to church life and finding his way around, he discovered the close tie-up between church and business. It grievously troubled him. He had thought that he had escaped from the snare of iniquity. Now the church was keeping it in business. He is only a new Christian, a babe in Christ. Are these people in his new fellowship serious? Are they really in business for the kingdom of God? They argue with him, produce their knowledge and their evidence. But he feels that there must be something phony about them. He is wrong. But he has not entered into their knowledge. His early keenness is stifled. He broods over his problems. He stays away from church some Sundays. He stays away. His private prayer is intermittent. It becomes rarer. It stops. And so does he. Stubborn "knowledge" would not help a troubled ignorance.

Again, a prominent Christian with large business interests has to have permanent legal advice. He has the most brilliant lawyer available and has close dealings with him almost every day. But the man is a notorious playboy who has charmed and ruined dozens of girls. One of his victims is converted and joins the church. In time she learns that the playboy is on the permanent staff of one of the pillars of the church. Everybody "knows" that he is consulted on nothing but legal matters. But the girl scents danger. What can happen with such a man on the loose? She is troubled for the reputation of the "pillar" and indeed for that of the church. Which girl in the employ of the "pillar" will be the next victim? Those with ' knowledge" laugh at her fears. Then the tragedy takes place. Who are these Christians who do not care? She is troubled; loses the spiritual glow; falls away; stays away; cynical; finished with it all.

The strong must care for the weak. The strong in faith must not take advantage of the weak in faith. The strong must leaven their knowledge with love. They must remember that example may be a more powerful influence than argument and that love may do more than knowledge. Watch your step! The knowledge which preserves you may ruin someone else.

If we follow this line, a "taste" of Paul's methods may have much to say to the modern church. (Cf. Rom. 14:1–23; 1 Cor. 10:14–33.)

In a revealing passage the apostle shows us how he read the Old Testament "for our admonition" (1 Cor. 10:1–13, KJV). The events recorded were not mere events, significant for the time only in which they took place. They were "typical," or "pattern-events." They happened but they were the sort of events which could happen to us.

We are so used to the thought of the Last Supper, the Lord's Supper recorded in the first three Gospels, that some of us tend to limit ourselves to the story given by the evangelists and to be surprised to find it in the Epistles. It might not have appeared there if abuses had not arisen in Corinth (10:14–22; 11:17–34). Paul said that when the church in Corinth gathered together it was not possible to eat the Lord's Supper. There is unseemly haste. Each man goes ahead and eats his own supper, with one man going short and another drunk. They are not without homes for eating and drinking, are they? Do they despise the church of God? Do they humiliate the have-nots? In an effective understatement, Paul says that he does not approve.

He proceeds to give his classical statement of the institution of the Supper. It takes us back to the Gospels and indicates how faithfully the apostle, years afterwards, was obeying the Lord's original command. It reminds us of the "breaking of bread" in the early days of the church (Acts 2:42, 46) as well as later (Acts 20:7, 11).

Paul held strong views about the communion service. It is

an act of obedience to the Lord. A man must test himself first. Then he should eat and drink. He should remember— clearly—who the Lord is and what he has done "for us." And he should "discern the body." Unworthy reception can be dangerous to health and even life. It is impossible to drink the cup of the Lord and the cup of demons. It is impossible logically, for one is incompatible with the other. It might prove impossible in fact, if we provoke the Lord to jealousy. We are not stronger than he is. We cannot be slaves to two owners.

Paul goes on to consider the question of spiritual "gifts." These are to be distinguished from what are sometimes called natural talents. As a result of heredity or environment or both, a man may have a great aptitude for playing the piano, great skill in carpentry or architectural design, or be a genius in mathematics. A gift comes to an individual from the Holy Spirit. It may possibly be the heightening of a natural talent, but without the addition of the actual gift it would have no spiritual vitality. As an example: Winston Churchill was a superb orator but he had no gift as a preacher.

Whether or not a gift is really a gift or only a natural talent, whether or not it comes from the Holy Spirit, it is to be judged by one great test. What is its possessor's attitude to Jesus Christ? Nobody with a gift of the Spirit curses our Lord, and nobody can confess him as Lord apart from the Holy Spirit who teaches him to do so (1 Cor. 12:1–31).

The Spirit distributes his gifts, and there is a variety of them. They differ in what, as a result of having a gift, a man can do, what he actually does and what he accomplishes. Yet though he has a gift, it is God who activates it. The man "uses" it, but ultimately God starts it working and keeps it working. When the gift is at work, it manifests the Spirit. A sympathetic and understanding observer does not say, "What a wonderful man! Look at what he is doing." He sees rather the Spirit being made manifest. Anyone with a spiritual eye sees him rather than the man. The purpose of the gift is not exhibition, certainly not the exhibition of the man. It is for the profit of all.

The gifts, we say, vary. One man speaks words of wisdom.

He has insight into a situation, can assess its meaning and possibilities and can give good advice. Another has knowledge which is denied to others—though it is not necessarily "secret" information. He just knows, and what he states is fact. Yet another man has faith. This at first is surprising: all Christians in the New Testament have faith. If they had no faith, they would not be Christians at all. Paul is clearly thinking of the exceptional man. Our Lord spoke of faith the size of a grain of mustard seed. Such "tiny" faith can grow. A small seed can grow when a speck of dust cannot. But in the meantime faith is small. But there are believing men who have a gift of faith which is rare. They walk more closely with God than most Christians. They pray more frequently. In one sense perhaps they never stop, not using words all the time, but "practicing the presence of God." Their prayers are answered, their requests granted, often on a stupendous scale and in almost romantic ways. By example and by experience they can help their relatively weaker brethren. Others have gifts of healing or "can get things done." One man is a prophet, not necessarily foretelling the future but making known the will of God. We recognize in him the authentic preacher—not merely the man who may occupy a pulpit. One man can distinguish between spirits and can keep the congregation from following a false trail. Yet another has the gift of tongues, whose ecstatic utterances are to be interpreted by his comrade with the gift of interpretation.

Some gifts are more spectacular than others and their possessors are subject to the temptation to parade them as if they were their own native powers. Paul knocks this idea on the head once and for all by his picture of the body and its limbs and organs. The foot, the hand, the ear, the eye, the head, have each a distinctive function, a specific task to be done. We do not normally walk on our hands, put food into our mouths with our feet or try to see with the ear. It is like that in the church: Paul says "so also is Christ." Each separate limb or organ of the body is necessary and each separate gifted man is necessary. The powerful preacher must not despise the sexton or janitor, or the leading "committee man." Many of us know—or can imagine—the chaos which

results on a Sunday morning when the building superin-
tendent has been involved in an accident and just does not
"turn up"; or we have experienced the drifting round the
subject and two hours' fruitless talk when the brains of the
committee are absent. The church needs "helps and govern-
ments"—men with a gift for helping or guiding others.

The "special" gift of faith is illustrated in our Lord's words
about the faith which moves mountains (Mark 11:23–25).

A century ago the discussion of "speaking in tongues"
might have been considered purely academic, having no practical relevance for the contemporary situation. It is not so
today. There has been an outburst of tongues all over the
world and we have to come to terms with it. Some Christians
are repelled by "enthusiasm"—an old criticism—and the "ir-
reverence" of the shouting and the noise. Others feel that it
is a sign of life renewed in a moribund, "churchy" society.
Yet others are impressed and deeply moved by the quiet
praise and prayer which ripples across the pew like a gentle
wave. Another, though a stranger to his denomination, can
form a close friendship in Christ with a Pentecostal minister.
We must see what the apostle has to teach us (1 Cor.
14:1–40).

Paul's long chapter may be summarized in a series of
"points." (1) He thanks God that he speaks in tongues more
than any of them. He thus knows the experience from the
inside. He can do it; he has done it; and does it (v. 18). He is
no mere theorizer.

(2) He wants all the Corinthian Christians to speak in
tongues; but he wants something else even more: that they
may prophesy. This reveals their relative importance.
Prophecy is the more important. "The man who prophesies
is greater than the man who speaks in tongues—unless he
interprets" (v. 5). The emphasis is still on prophecy but it is
now ecstatic preaching—a sermon in the power of the Spirit,
with some speaking in tongues and its explanation. It is still
preaching. If there is no interpreter, the man who speaks in
tongues must be silent in church (v. 28).

(3) Prophecy is more important because it edifies, and
everything must be done with a view to edification. The

church is to be built up. The preacher builds, encourages and stimulates, and consoles (vv. 1–4, 26).

(4) The prophecy of all would be a sure sign of the real presence of God. If all prophesy, the unbeliever present is unmasked by all, examined by all; the secrets of his heart are clear. Thus exposed he will fall on his face and worship God, frankly confessing that "God is among you in very deed" (vv. 24–25).

(5) In sharp contrast, if the whole church assembles and they all speak with tongues, the outsider who comes in will think he has entered a lunatic asylum.

(6) The essential factor is the mind, or reason. It is possible to pray with the "spirit," which Paul here seems to regard as the "ego minus thought." He prefers to speak five words with his mind when in church than tens of thousands in a tongue. His motive is to give instruction by making himself understood, to edify or build (vv. 13–19). Just as preaching in tongues (point 2) needs interpretation—or the preacher must be silent in church—so praying in tongues needs interpretation; otherwise there is no understanding and no edification. Praying in tongues without interpretation is for the ear of God alone and best done in private. It is the Word which builds (Acts 20:32).

(7) In spite of Paul's critical—though not unsympathetic —attitude, he sees a place for speaking with tongues. He applies a text from the prophet Isaiah in a different context (Isa. 28:11–12) and draws an inference. Tongues are a sign to the unbelieving; not the unbelieving outsider who comes in and thinks everybody has gone mad but the unbelieving "insider." Tongues are God's rebuke to an unbelieving congregation. (1 Cor. 14:21–22). Strive for prophecy but do not hinder speaking in tongues (v. 39). The tongues will rebuke and the prophecy or preaching will build.

There has been much criticism of Pentecostalism. If the modern church is to be faithful, attention should be given to Paul's message. The outburst of tongues is God's rebuke to his church of today. It has shown hesitation and unbelief, with—in some quarters at least—little appetite for the Word. God has given what many people asked for: the absence of mind, the absence of Christian instruction, the absence of the preaching of the Word. The church has looked to gimmicks and God has given it one! Let us accept the rebuke and seek afresh the preaching of the Word which builds in faith and character and fellowship.

In passing from the gifts of the Spirit in their variety to the gift of tongues, we had to omit one of the best known parts of Paul's writings. It is appropriate for us to consider it at this stage. Some earnest enthusiasts for speaking in tongues have given the impression, rightly or wrongly, that a man who cannot speak in tongues is a second-class Christian, and can never be more until he does speak in tongues. They forget that there are diversities of gifts: one man has one gift and another man has another. "They do not all speak in tongues do they?" (1 Cor. 12:30). Yet there is an activity open to all.

Paul's "hymn to love" (13:1–13) is celebrated. However necessary the modern translations may be in the interests of deeper understanding, they have lost the rhythm and music of the King James Version. Think of "charity [say it slowly] suffereth long and is ki-i-ind." The rhythm pleases our ears and arrests our attention, and the long drawn out "kind" illustrates in sound the length of love's patience. We shall not here attempt an exposition of this noble chapter but rather draw attention to some possibilities of interpretation.

The subject is "love." It is sometimes asked, whose love? Is it God's love? Perhaps it is; and yet it seems in part at least to think of human love. Does God have faith to remove mountains? Is it seemly to say that God does not envy or is not puffed up? Love is considered in the abstract and it is instructive as a spiritual exercise to take out the abstract term *love* and replace it with the word *Jesus*. "Jesus suffers long and is kind. . . ." Next, think of some much loved saint of the local congregation, known by all for his Christian life and character. Put his name in, instead of "love." "Mr. X. does not behave himself unseemly, seeks not his own, is not easily provoked, thinketh no evil. Mr. X does not rejoice in iniquity but rejoices in the truth. He bears all things . . . and endures all things. He never fails."

Now comes the test. Let each Christian insert his own name as a challenge to his own discipleship. "I seek not my own (selfish?); I am not easily provoked (do I keep my temper?); I do not rejoice when another man crashes morally (complacency? gossip?)." This is an almost frightening experiment. Jesus is the very embodiment of love. Mr. X is the disciple trying to show it. I am—what? Am I even trying?

Paul's great resurrection chapter (15:1–58) will be known to many from their attendance at funeral services. He begins with the gospel which he had preached at Corinth and which his readers had received. He sums it up in its important points, which tally with the preaching of the gospel in the Acts and indeed with St. Mark's Gospel as a whole, and dwells on the resurrection appearances of Christ. Then he goes in to the attack.

If it is proclaimed that Christ has been raised from the dead, how can some among you say that there is no such thing as the resurrection of the dead? We expect unbelievers to be consistent and not to believe. We expect some of them to scoff. But "some among you"? Denial in the church itself? Instead of merely offering a denunciation, the apostle draws out the consequences. All right: there is no such thing as resurrection; have you considered what this involves? Let us work it out. It follows that Christ has not been raised. Then our preaching has nothing in it—and your faith has nothing in it either. Our disguise has been penetrated: we are perjurers. We affirmed that God had raised Christ—and he hadn't. Do you see what this means for you? It is not just a nice point to be discussed in theological seminaries or some other place as irrelevant to you as the moon. It has practical consequences for you. Your faith is futile. It never did anything for you. You are still in your sins. And it never did anything for your friends either. They are dead, gone, perished. You will never see them again.

What a situation! We have put our hope in Christ only "for the duration," as they say in wartime. We have no eternal hope. We might as well be downright secularists. We are of all men most—not miserable but—to be pitied. We staked our all on him. To use the language of the world which is now our only home: we put all our eggs into one basket; we put all we had on one horse. It was the biggest and most tragic mistake of our lives.

"But now" (another sigh of relief; cf. Rom. 3:21): Paul turns from the necessary argument to the triumphant fact. Christ is risen from the dead, the first fruits of those who have fallen asleep—through Jesus (1 Thess. 4:14). He goes on to expound the Advent hope and the manner of our future resurrection, touching on a paradox, our "spiritual body." Then he takes a surprising turn.

We tend to think of the "collection" in a church service as rather an intrusion into the worship. In some churches they "get it out of the way" before the edifying sermon. Let us forget "filthy lucre" and concentrate on things divine! Paul's writings do not encourage such a view. He knew nothing of chapter and verse divisions and after his sublime treatment of the theme of our Lord's resurrection and our own resurrection he said: "Now concerning the collection. . . ." He was not stepping down from a high theme to a regrettable earthly necessity. He was not "stepping down" at all. He was just "going on." Our Lord spoke of "the altar which sanctifies the gift" (Matt. 23:19), and Paul would understand and sympathize if we spoke of "the resurrection which sanctifies the collection."

For the collection was not then and is not now a "whip-round," a clubbing together to raise a bit of money for something or other. It was an offering inspired by Christian fellowship and love for poor Christians in Jerusalem (1 Cor. 16:1–4). It must have astonished any observers at that time to see Gentiles sending money to help Jews. And it did not come only from Corinth. The churches of Galatia were involved. The churches of Macedonia clamored to be allowed to contribute (2 Cor. 8:4). It was not a case of a leading ecclesiastic going round the churches begging. The Macedonians did the begging!

This puts "the collection" on to an entirely new footing. It is not mere money, though of course it is and has to be money. It is a gift from the Christian heart. We love because he first loved us. We give, because he first gave (2 Cor. 8:9). The altar sanctifies the gift. The resurrection of our Lord exalts the collection of cash from people to an offering of love from Christ's redeemed believers. It does not pay for their redemption. It is an act of thanksgiving that they have received the gracious gifts of redemption. And it helps their fellow members who have likewise entered into life in Christ.

We have studied the apostle's First Epistle to the Corinthians in some breadth and depth. Before we leave Corinth, we shall take a few more samples, a few sips here and there, to complete the savor. It is easy to misunderstand Paul's teaching or to distort it. "Shall we continue in sin, that grace may abound?" (Rom. 6:1, KJV). He is the apostle of free grace and of justification by faith. Believers are no longer under the law. Yet he can say that circumcision and uncircumcision are nothing, "but keeping God's commandments" everything (1 Cor. 7:19). These have now become "the law of Christ" (Gal. 6:2).

The apostle's own ideal and practice sheds a welcome light on the nature of the ministry. All pastors should pay attention to it, especially those who shrink from obtruding their own personality. God "comforts us in all our affliction, so that we may be able to comfort men in any affliction by means of the comfort with which we ourselves are comforted by God" (2 Cor. 1:4). Some are critical of "preaching their own experience," and their reluctance is a wholesome safeguard against a subjective emphasis on their own experience and nothing else. But how does God "comfort"? Paul would not omit "the comfort of the scriptures" (Rom. 15:4). This changes the picture. The minister should not try to share his own feelings of relief. How can you share "feelings"? But he can point to appropriate scriptures and say that in the mercy of God he has tried them, proved them and found them to be God's own comfort to him. By sharing the scriptures which he himself has proved, he can share his own comfort—and comfort others. "We speak what we know and give as testi-

mony what we have seen" (John 3:11). The scriptures point
to Christ, in whom God is known. Through the scriptures
Paul encounters the comforting God in the comforting Christ.
He tells of the comfort which he has thus found, and thus
comforts others.

But the ministry is not all "comfort." This is perhaps intermittent, coming to the fore in times of deep distress and
sorrow. But when the sorrow has been outlived, what then?
Paul shows us one permanent aspect of the ministry. "It is
not that we are lording it over your faith; we are helpers of
your joy" (2 Cor. 1:24). The aim is to work with them and
not against them; for them and not to their disadvantage; to
speed them on and not to impede them. It is not to satisfy
them at any cost and in any way as long as it will "work." It
is to sustain, enlarge and deepen their joy in the Lord.

For his task the minister has endless resources at his dis-
posal. Joy is increased when grace is received, and grace is
still coming, as the salutations at the beginning of the epistles
testify. It is the minister's business to give grace, and he has
ample supplies on which to draw. It is surpassing. It goes
beyond all speech and outbids all rivals. We might imagine
that after writing the Epistle to the Romans, Paul could
think that he had given a full account of the grace of God,
and in a sense he had. But in the end he knew that he was
engaged in an impossible task. The gift of God is so rich and
varied that in the end it cannot be described, still less expounded, and lesser still explained. Thanks be to God for his
gift that can never be finally stated, illustrated or expounded.
This is both the despair and the hope of the minister. He
knows that he is inadequate to the task of preaching and
teaching the unsearchable riches of Christ, not necessarily
because he is no preacher—he may have brilliant gifts—but
because of the inexhaustible nature of his subject. But this is
his encouragement and his glory: he himself may "run dry,"
but his subject never will. He has always more to say of
Christ (2 Cor. 9:14–15).

If all is as it should be, we can draw up a "plan of opera-
tions" and see the minister's place in it. Christ himself sows
the seed (Matt. 13:37) and proclaims the light (Acts 26:23).

He speaks in his minister (2 Cor. 13:3), and "he who hears you, hears me" (Luke 10:16). Is it surprising that the minister can, does and should give comfort and joy to Christ's own people?

The Second Epistle to the Corinthians closes with words which are familiar to many, though they may not all be able to locate them in print. "The grace of the Lord Jesus Christ and the love of God and the fellowship of the Holy Spirit be, is, will be, with you all." The absence of a verb in the Greek allows a wideness of interpretation.

The Epistle to the Galatians

If Paul faced a series of problems in writing to Corinth, he saw a concentrated danger in the churches of Galatia. He wrote the Epistle to the Galatians in a white heat of indignation. His work there had been subject to interference. This in itself does not explain his anger. Interference may sometimes be anticipated as natural. In politics, if the opposition suddenly comes to power, it "interferes" with the developing policy of its predecessors. In sport, the man who scores the equalizing goal certainly interferes with the whole of the other team. In a sense the apostle himself had interfered in the religious life of Judaism and of heathenism. But the present situation was different. The interference was deliberate and deadly. The point of its sword was at the heart of the Galatians. They were the victims of troublemakers who were distorting the gospel of Christ (Gal. 1:6–7). This alone can explain his astonishment at their behavior. It is more than the schoolmaster's "I'm surprised at you, Jones," for some trifling mistake or misdemeanor. Paul is thunderstruck. His converts were unsettled in mind and were being coerced, forced (6:12), by enemies.

Imagine their plausible talk. You have been listening to this Paul. He has some good ideas: he remembers Jesus Christ. But he has much to learn. His attitude to the law is quite wrong. Now we are telling you the truth of the gospel. . . . There is a modern ring about it all. We have seen churches with centuries of Christian service behind them assailed by modern heretics who have distorted the gospel and unsettled thousands.

Paul is not worried just because his nose has been put out of joint. He is not suffering from wounded pride. The Galatians had received him as an angel of God, as Christ Jesus, whose messenger he was. Where is that deep satisfaction now? (4:14–15). They are in grievous danger. They are on the move—away from God. They are making for another gospel —which is no gospel. He does not say that they are deserting God for another god or that they are leaving the gospel for a false gospel. They are leaving the One who called them, and he called them when the grace of Christ was preached in the gospel. To take up with a distorted gospel is not merely a theological change of mind. It is the desertion of God himself —whose voice they had heard in their hearts as a divine call which they had joyously answered. To abandon the gospel in which God is known is to abandon God himself (1:6–7). It merits judgment (5:10) and the curse (1:8–9), even if the "preacher" of such a distorted gospel is an angel from heaven.

They cannot complain that they were misled in the first place by being shown a picture out of focus. So vivid had been the apostle's preaching, so clear the portrait of Christ crucified which he had painted with his verbal brush, that they had had vision enough. It had been as arresting as the advertisement billboards which placard our main highways and compel our attention even as we swiftly pass: how huge is their lettering and how sharp and colorful the scene they present!

Now the Galatians' vision is dim. Some wizard spell has all but shut their eyes (3:1), foolish as they are. They are flagging in their discipleship (5:7). They are not going forward but backward. They once knew God and were known by him, in all his power and wealth. How can they be converted backward; how can they desire to start up again their original slavery? Do they love their bonds? For bondage it is (4:8–11). They had each escaped from slavery to sonship, with an inheritance in prospect (4:7). Christ had liberated them—for liberty. Enjoy it! Stand firm in it! Don't be entangled again in slavery, to be pulled hither and yon against your will (5:1).

Are they so stupid as not to realize what they are letting themselves in for? Christ will profit them nothing. Every man who lets himself be circumcised takes on the obligation to keep the law in its entirety. Read as a sample the Book of Leviticus: a painful start (circumcision) and a boring burden which even the people brought up to it could not tolerate (Acts 15:10), let alone successfully obey. Christ will be no help to them. For it is not a question of Christ and the law, but Christ or the law. They have fallen out of the realm of grace, not by a slip which made them lose their balance and crash. They fell because they jumped—and their parachute failed to open (5:2–4).

They had attained to life through faith. Through faith comes justification, sonship, reception of the Holy Spirit. Through faith they become members of the lineage of Abraham and heirs (3:2–7, 14, 24–29). Why change from grace to law, from faith to works? Why revert to the immaturity, the slavery of infancy? It is as bad as that (4:1–7). Before Christ came they were under a sort of tutor (3:24). Why go back to him, no true teacher but merely the slave who took the children to school? Why suffer the painful circumcision which does nothing for them? There is something better than that! Have they forgotten the new creation? They have been slacking. They should take their thought away from circumcision and from distinctions which avail nothing, and come back to a faith which does not ease off but is operative through love (5:6; 6:15). Then, with faith firm and working, they are in position for "keeping the commandments of God" (1 Cor. 7:19).

If they are so concerned with law, their priorities must be right. The whole law is summed up in one word, *love* (5:14), and love is the fruit of the Spirit (5:22–23). It "grows" from the Spirit, as it were; it is organically connected, not laboriously produced in a factory; grown and harvested, not constructed. Paul is concerned with both seed and soil. Choose the right seed. What you sow you will reap: sow wheat and you will reap wheat; sow law and you will reap law, and the condemnation which it brings; sow faith and the harvest will be eternal life. Sow in the soil of flesh, which is where law operates, and from it you will reap ruin and destruction. Sow in the Spirit, and from the Spirit of grace you will have the harvest of eternal life.

Paul argues passionately—and affectionately—from a strong position. He was the object and bearer of divine revelation (1:15–16). He did not receive the gospel from any man and was not taught it. It came to him through the revelation of Jesus Christ (1:11–12). His office and work of apostle did not originate in men. He was not elected by a congregation or appointed by apostles or other church officers, however eminent or holy. It was not transmitted by God through a man by the laying-on of ordaining hands (cf. Acts 9:12, 17). It came through the ascended Lord, Jesus Christ, and God the Father who raised him from the dead (1:1). Paul was led by revelation (2:2).

His position was independent. In the early part of the Epistle he shows that his conversion was well-known, as well as his corresponding behavior before and after conversion. He had been an advanced legalist, persecuting the church. He became an evangelist, the apostle to the Gentiles. Those who did not know him but heard about his career praised God for the change. He frankly reviews his association with prominent leaders of the church, making it perfectly plain that he was not seeking correction or confirmation of his gospel, approbation of his work or authority to do it. He had received from God all that was necessary. There was fellowship in Christ, as was natural and right. They and he were alike believers and workers in the kingdom of God. At one point Paul rebuked Peter to his face. Independent as he was, they recognized him. God had given him the gospel and a field of labor. The Epistle to the Galatians shows us the faithfulness with which he carried out his apostolate.

The Epistle to the Ephesians

If in Galatians we see free grace defended, in the Epistle to the Ephesians we have a summary of the gospel. This leads us to expect some sort of outline, a "skeleton" of main points.

This is the very reverse of the truth. Ephesians sums up Paul's thought and elaborates it in six chapters of compact statement. Their doctrinal "density" is high.

After a short preliminary greeting, less than a third of the length of the salutation with which he began the Epistle to the Romans, Paul plunges into his subject. He makes up for his initial brevity in a "monster of a sentence," ten verses long. We gain the impression that he could not get the words out quickly enough, so much is there to be told. Christian truth is rich in content and it comes pouring out from the apostle's richly stored mind. He "cannot but speak" (cf. Acts 4:20). The truth simmered and fermented within him, the pressure mounted, and there was no safety valve to relieve it. Once the opening had been made, nothing could stop him. It would be like trying to stem the fireman's hose with your thumb.

He begins with a general statement, with a play upon words which is not a facetious pun but a quiet way of pointing to two activities, each going in the opposite direction. "Blessed be the God and Father of our Lord Jesus Christ, who blessed us with all spiritual blessing in the heavenlies in Christ" (1:3). God is infinitely blessed in himself. He is the sum of all perfection. If anyone in the whole universe should be respected, reverenced, praised and worshiped, he is the One. "Blessed *be* the God. . . ." Our thanksgiving, our praise, our blessing ought to be directed towards him. This is one "direction."

In the other direction God has blessed us. He has given us infinite good. What is it? He blessed us "with all spiritual blessing." Nothing has been omitted: note the "all." The word sometimes conveys the idea of "nothing but." God has blessed us with nothing but spiritual blessing. There is no defect in quality. It is all first class and the quantity is infinite. In sparing not his own Son, God in principle gave us everything (Rom. 8:32). His gift can never be endangered. It is "in the heavenlies." Earthly wealth can never be absolutely safe. It can be relatively safe, or to what purpose do we have armies and police forces? But it can never be safe in the absolute sense, safe without exception, without qualification, just "safe, period." Moth and rust are always ready to attack. Men take their opportunity to embezzle. Thieves plan. Burglars polish their housebreaking tools. Robbers have their clubs or guns in their hands. Banks may fail, revolutions break out, or land be occupied. Money may lose all its value by inflation. After World War I a man in Germany took paper money in a wheelbarrow to buy a loaf of bread—and found himself still short of cash to buy it. Our treasure is safe, located where it is (cf. Matt. 6:19-21). Nothing is omitted; nothing is shoddy; nothing is in danger. We need not concern ourselves with derisive comments about "pie in the sky." That is where the pie is, with a biblical interpretation of "sky," not a worldly one. And it must not be forgotten that the heavenly pie has an earthly hors d'oeuvre. "Your heavenly Father knows that you need all these things. Seek first his kingdom and righteousness and all these things will come to you in addition" (Matt. 6:32-33).

And the gift is not depersonalized. It is not a "thing." Grace itself is not a commodity. It is embodied in Christ. God has blessed us with all spiritual blessing for he has blessed us with Christ. In him we find all the blessings. We might think that this is a climax, and in a sense it is. But given a man like Paul and a subject like Christ, what can we expect? Think of the man who preached all night at Troas and nonstop at Ephesus night and day for three years. It is not the story of a man who goes droning on, half asleep like the congregation in front of him, grinding it out, churning it out, staying where he is and doing what he does because he cannot see the door marked "exit." Christ: what a subject! Off he goes, running, jumping, leaping, until he arrives breathless and panting at the twelfth verse. What to other men might be obstacles he takes in his stride. Look at them as he hurtles over them. They are not obstacles at all but familiar ground, joyously once more to be traversed. Christ: what does it mean? What is implied? Why, election, its purpose, our holiness and blamelessness; predestination and its purpose, adoption through Jesus Christ; grace and our experience of it, all by the dear will of God, to be praised for its very glory; redemption, the blood of Christ, forgiveness; grace again, its priceless value and infinite quantity, coming to us like a swelling tide; wisdom, nothing but wisdom, and the eternal plan and purpose for everything in heaven and earth to be under the sway of Christ; our own admission to the purpose of him whose will is ever active to implement our blessed foreordination; the praise of his glory from such as us whose hope is already set firm in Christ.

You who heard the word of truth and believed it, the gospel of your salvation, were in consequence sealed with the promised Holy Spirit. And he in all his fullness is but the beginning, the first part of the inheritance which is to follow.

Nothing can stop Paul. Having heard of his readers' individual faith and love, he does not cease to give thanks for them and to pray for them. God has yet more gifts for them in Christ, and the apostle ecstatically describes the gifts, contrasting their former distance and death with their present nearness and life. Blessing in the heavenlies? Christ is seated there and so are you!

For God had quickened them, brought them from death to life, raised them and seated them in the heavenlies. By his grace he had saved them and kept them safe. We have said that Paul could not be "stopped." We should further observe that he cannot be cramped. He ranges far and wide with a largeness of conception which gives him—and us—room to maneuver. And he cannot be blindfolded or put into blinkers. Physically he may have been short-sighted—his "peering" at men suggests that he did not see too well—but spiritually he had long sight, wide sight and insight. His breadth of conception and of vision was allied to a vividness of imagination and of imaginative expression. He includes heaven as well as earth, the future as well as the present. Our warfare is not merely against flesh and blood, not merely the sum total of the human population. The forces of hostility are vaster. We fight against rules and authorities, against world-rulers of this darkness, against transcendent powers which work for evil in the spiritual realm. Paul did not minimize the foe against us and he did not minimize what we have for us. God gave Christ to the church as Head over everything, everything both inside and outside the church. It is as if an enthusiastic student cried out with joy, "Our principal is head of the government as well!" Over the spacious realm of nature, the expansive universe itself; over the long course of history, with all its apparent chances and its obvious changes; and over his own church: Christ rules as Lord in full control. Nature, history and grace, Christ is supreme in all.

And the church is ever growing, a huge building with additions made section by section, which proves to be not a mere building at all but a temple in which God himself dwells. We have spoken of Paul's imagination: he changes his figure of a building into that of a body. The church is the Body of Christ. His life is in it, and through its limbs and organs he carries out his will. The apostle can bring the two figures together and speak of building the body. Further the church is the Bride of Christ, always distinct from him but never separate from him, never losing her identity yet still absorbed in him. Even with this imaginative man, language all but fails. He prays that his readers may grasp the breadth and length and height and depth of the love of Christ. It will not elude their grasp but it is too big to hold. All the saints together, pooling their experiences, telling one another of all that Christ in his love has done and is doing for them, putting the knowledge of each into the shared treasury of all, will not have the final and full knowledge of his love. They know it— in part. All eternity will not exhaust its fullness. They will always be learning more, for the love of Christ surpasses knowledge. If we, as well as Paul, exercise our imagination, we might think of a transatlantic telephone cable. Imagine a man on land, trying to haul it in. He keeps on pulling, yard after yard, mile after mile . . . and still it comes. It covers the whole Atlantic. In theory, but only in theory (!), he could pull it all in, in time. But not with the infinite love of Christ. Grasp it for ever, and it still comes.

Paul's canvas is large. He needs a large one. How could he describe the power of God? He is able to do beyond all measure, with no adequate comparison, infinitely, all that he ever wills. His power is greater than our neediest prayers at any time could require, vaster than the thought or imagination of a genius.

Yet for all the size of the canvas, Paul can draw with the nicety of a mapping pen. He can think of the individual. On the one side we have the surpassing wealth of God's grace embodied in Christ, surpassing our knowledge and its grasp. On the other side he can pray for the strengthening of the readers by the penetration of the Holy Spirit into the inward man, into the very self; that is, that Christ may take up residence in human hearts. He comes in "through faith." Faith is individually exercised. It may indeed be in a context of fellowship, but each man has to believe for himself. So the man used to a large canvas can draw a tiny "map" as well.

What does he draw? He depicts a simple, humble man, with no money, no position, little intellect to speak of, shabby clothes, a mean lodgment and no influence: even he can be host to Christ in his infinite love and grace. This is not coming down from the sublime to the ridiculous. It is putting vast grace precisely where—if not where it "belongs" at any rate where—God meant it to be. Where there is desperate human need, and a cry for help, Jesus comes.

The apostle urges his readers to walk worthily of their call, not to walk as Gentiles walk (though Ephesian Gentiles used so to walk!), and to avoid the sins which it would be disgraceful even to mention—a lesson in reticence which our age might well take to heart. He gives some directions for specific classes—wives, husbands, children, fathers, slaves and slaveowners. We might at first wonder if Paul is here very much coming down to earth. Moral instructions are hardly sublime. But that is just the point.

We have had a variety of figures of speech and we must now introduce another one. Paul has not abandoned with regret his great exposition and illustration of the love and grace of God in Christ. He still believes it all. And he is not passing on from one chapter to the next, as it were, implying that "I have said all I need to about the grace of God. Now we must leave that for another subject. We must consider your moral duty." He is not abandoning the grace, even temporarily, when he speaks of duty. He is bringing it with him. All that he has so richly said about God's grace in Christ he is *harnessing* for the duty of walking worthily. There is the general duty of all Christians, to love God and to love neighbor. And there are also specific duties. Some may overlap but some are distinct. The duty of a father differs from that of a child. The father should provide, the child is to be tended. The duty of a wife is not that of a slave, and the duty of a slaveowner is not that of a child. All God's infinite grace in Christ is available to inspire and help in the discharge of duty. The "harnessing" of grace is the new figure.

Apart from a few "messages" of the conclusion the letter ends with request for prayer for Paul's preaching ministry. He is still "unstoppable."

The Epistle to the Philippians

Paul is growing older all the time and it is interesting to reflect on the effect of age on the theologian or preacher. A minister once told his colleagues at a meeting of the ministerial association that "the older I get, the fewer things I believe." It might be quite innocent: he might mean that he had learned to concentrate on the great doctrines and to preach on the great texts, and not to be diverted in study and pulpit to secondary themes. It might be innocent, though I am not sure. However this particular question is settled, Paul had no desire to "cut down" his articles of belief. On the contrary, the more he could claim for Christ the better. We have already noticed the "density" of the Epistle to the Ephesians. It is packed with thought. The Epistle to the Philippians is not so dense, but it does not betray any thinning out of the faith—as if the apostle had planted some seeds of lettuce and had to thin out the first shoots in order to give room for the remainder to grow!

As we read Philippians we feel how mellow Paul has become. There is a warmth of affection which reminds us of a "pastor-emeritus" writing to a church to which he had ministered for twenty years, known and loved by all. Even so, we must not fall into the trap of thinking that the apostle was now no more than a dear old man, loving everybody, trusting everybody, and blind to every fault and heedless of any deviations from Christian truth. He does not here strike us preeminently as a fighting controversialist, passionately defending the true faith against vigorous opposition and treacherous teachers of false doctrine. But he is still at his post in defense of the gospel, and he has not gone back on the doctrines which he had earlier preached so forcefully and so faithfully. He can still repudiate a righteousness of his own, achieved by his own efforts to obey the law. He still has a righteousness based on faith, a righteousness which came from God as a gift through his faith in Christ (3:9). He can still ardently expect the Second Advent (3:20) and wonder if it will happen so soon that he will not have to be resurrected from the dead (3:11). He does not lump everybody together in "one happy family." He can still speak—with tears—of the enemies of the cross of Christ, of their disgraceful manner of life and their final perdition (3:18–19).

He is still the evangelist, still sensitive to the opportunities for evangelism and rejoicing that others besides himself have taken the opportunities. Even his imprisonment has furthered the work. Most of the local Christians have been spurred on, not intimidated, by his bonds, and have the courage to go on speaking the Word of God without fear. There are disharmonies to be sure which did not escape him and which undoubtedly caused him pain. Some loved him, recognized the cause of his imprisonment and the work which he was still doing, and gave him their "support" by preaching Christ. Others had mixed motives. They were envious of the apostle's record and prominence, jealous of him and ambitious for themselves. A "row" or "church bother" would not have displeased them. Does this fellow think he can preach? He's not the only one. We'll show him! And so they proclaim Christ—and think that by so doing they will teach him a lesson and turn the screw a bit tighter.

Here is one of the points which reveal the greatness of Paul. Resentment might have been born and a period of brooding started. But his dominant purpose was not weakened; his breadth of vision was not narrowed. Their motives in preaching Christ are mixed, are they? This does not bother me. Why so? Why, because in every way Christ is being proclaimed. Some may preach him with the side purpose of putting me in my place; some may preach him with the sole purpose of—preaching Christ. In either case, Christ is preached. Good! I rejoice in it and shall continue to rejoice in it. A lesser man would have taken the huff. Not so Paul: "for me to live is Christ"; all else is secondary (1:12–21).

Broad is his vision and broad likewise are his sympathies. He would never be other than an apostle and would never resign the authority of his apostleship. But he was not always harping on it, as if his privilege and destiny were different from those of his readers. They and he drank at the same well and were sustained by the same food. Through Christ they were closely related, he to the Philippians and they to him. He "had them in his heart." They were all his copartners, co-sharers, co-participators in grace. Even an apostle needs salvation and he enjoyed precisely the same salvation as his readers did—salvation by grace.

Both parties received the same salvation and both were engaged in the same activity. The readers were not apostles, but as Christian believers they continued in worship and witness, and they had their adversaries. It was no doubt on a much smaller scale, but they were doing and suffering what the apostle did and suffered, and it was all for the sake of Christ. Paul and the Philippians were characterized by clear purpose, strenuous effort and militant opposition. They had seen him go into action in their own city and were hearing how he was continuing the struggle in prison. It was not his own private affair, distinguished and glorious though it was. They were involved in the same conflict as Paul was. He and they were both fighting the one same good fight of faith (1:7, 27–30).

They fought on different fronts in the one war, he in his prison and they in their city. No doubt his sermons were longer than theirs! It had become clear for anybody to see that he was in bonds for being a Christian (1:13). They were shining in a world of crooks and perverts like stars in a dark night (2:15–16). Both were holding fast to the word of life and both were offering it to dead souls around them.

Paul did indeed have his private pressures. He had had so much of Christ that he longed for more. To go on living on earth was just—Christ. Suddenly to die would be sheer gain. But there were people here below who needed him. Hence he was "in a strait betwixt two" (1:23, KJV)—under pressure from two quarters. He resembled a member of the House of Representatives who is at the mercy of two opposing lobbies. The "Greek" lobby says to him: "If you support military aid to Turkey, you will never be reelected." The other lobby says: "If you deny help to Turkey you will damage NATO (North Atlantic Treaty Organization) and be unpatriotic." Which exercises the stronger pressure on the unfortunate representative?

It is like this with Paul, and he reveals with deep feeling how he is torn apart. One "lobby" says: "Think of your own personal preference. You want to be off to what is infinitely better, to be with Christ. Make that your choice." The other lobby points to duty as opposed to preference, to the necessities of the situation. Paul's ministry here has not ended. Don't resign—even to go (not to another church but) to heaven.

The choice does not rest with Paul but with divine providence. But we can see into the heart of this devout man and the wear and tear of lofty preference and hard duty, the longing to "come apart and rest" with Christ, which is a legitimate aspiration, and the stern call to remain at his post like a weary sentry who must keep awake for the sake of his comrades in arms. The final choice was not to be made by the disciple, but he endured all the emotional strain as if the choice were his. Many a pastor can enter in with understanding. I want to move; I need a change; but there is work to be done here that only I can do. I must not leave yet.

There is a continuity and consistency in Paul's religious experience which we should not fail to notice. He had told the Galatians that "I am no longer living but Christ lives in me" (Gal. 2:20). The life he does actually live is in faith in the Son of God. At heart it does not differ from "to live is Christ" (Phil. 1:21). Now in a real sense Christ is absent. He has ascended and is exalted to the right hand of God in heaven. Paul can even think of being absent from the Lord (2 Cor. 5:6-9). How then can he say that to live is Christ? He means more than that he is always thinking about him. Christ is always "with him." He does not come and go away, and then come again and go away again, and keep on coming and going. He stays. But how can he, if he is in heaven? Paul finds the presence of the absent Christ in the Holy Spirit. He speaks of the supply of the Spirit of Jesus Christ (1:19). He can refer in Galatians to "the One who supplies you with the Spirit" (Gal. 3:5), almost "the One who keeps on supplying." The same thought is expressed in Ephesians in the imperative "keep on being filled with the Spirit" (Eph. 5:18).

The breakdown of language here is of great significance. Christ is always with his people and he is with them through the Holy Spirit. The Spirit has been given and received. Yet he is being constantly "supplied" and believers are told to be constantly filled with the Spirit. It reminds us of everyday occurrences. We "fill up" with gas, even when the tank is almost empty. But we "top up" the battery with water. The Ephesians are always to be "topped up" with the Spirit. He is, so to speak, continually coming to his people. Some of us have had a stream running through our garden. The fresh water is constantly coming. If it did not, it would cease to be a stream. It would become just a muddy channel and finally a dry one—no more than a long, dry, trench. The water is always there—because it is always coming.

When is the Spirit received by believers? Some say at conversion and some say at baptism or confirmation. Some add to this and speak of a "second blessing" or the baptism of the Holy Spirit. Paul would not deny these interpretations— except possibly the use of the term *baptism*—but he would want to add to them. The Holy Spirit (through whom the absent Christ is present) is always present because he is always coming. He is a river rather than a well.

The apostle lays some emphasis on the inner life. He has much to say about thinking or having an attitude. His "mental exercise" about his readers is right (1:7). He wants them to have the same attitude, to be of one mind, to agree (2:2; 4:2). Their attitude in company should be the same as that which they have on their knees in private (cf. 2:5). The mature should maintain a certain turn of mind; a different view will be corrected by divine revelation (3:15). Some dwell on earthly things (3:19). Their mental home is the world. It is far better to keep their minds on all that is true, sublime, just and pure; on all that is lovely and whose tone is high; on all that is excellent and praiseworthy (4:8). Journalists, entertainers and politicians might well take the lesson to heart.

The Philippians had sent a gift to Paul and he rejoiced that their thought for him had flowered again (4:10). The Epistle is regarded by some as Paul's "receipt." We must not think of a formal statement ("paid with thanks") to "clear the church treasurer's books." Even so the letter is an acknowledgment, penned with wisdom and affection. The erstwhile blameless legalist (3:6) could have signed an office chit by way of receipt, but those days are far behind. The man who still heard the call of God in his soul (3:14) could have given a formal receipt if necessary; but he would have sent a covering letter, from one Christian to others, from a pastor who loved his flock to a people who returned his love with deeds, from a man who sent spiritual gifts in thanks for material ones. All this Paul did, to our own enrichment. It is a model "thank you" letter.

The Epistle to the Colossians

At first sight the Epistle to the Colossians seems to be very different from that to the Philippians. We are less inclined to warm our hands at its fireside, less drawn into the inner circle of its intimacy. It has a certain austerity which is missing from Philippians. Yet it should fill us with the warmth of worship: it contains a classic statement concerning the Person of Christ. It would be an exaggeration to say that its doctrine is an advance on that of Philippians. Its teaching about Christ does not go further than Philippians. It unfolds it. The deep implications of Philippians 2:5–11 are drawn out for us to see.

We often speak today of a man's "image." It is said that politicians are careful to preserve their public image intact, untarnished. Their image tells us how men look on them, how they "see" them. Now God has his image. Idolators like to see their god, but graven images have been forbidden by God in the Second Commandment (Exod. 20:4). Man is in the image of God (Gen. 1:26–27) but the image is marred. God himself is invisible. It was one of the puzzles of the heathen that the Jews were very religious but nobody had ever seen their god. Now he can be seen. Christ is "the image of God the Invisible" (Col. 1:15) and the image is not marred at all.

He is the First-born of all creation. This vivid figure of speech does not mean that Christ was created. The metaphorical use is not new. The first-born is obviously prior in time, but rank is also implied, a fact which makes the metaphor apt. Moses was to tell Pharaoh, "This is what the Lord says: Israel is my son, my first-born" (Exod. 4:22). Christ is thus prior to, and has authority over, all creation. This is clear from what immediately follows. He is First-born of all creation *because* in him everything was created, everything in heaven and on earth, seen and unseen—persons, including angels, "things," relations, natural laws, values.

Thus our Lord has a commanding relationship to the whole universe. He is the original Word or *Logos* (John 1:1–5), the very Wisdom of God (Prov. 8:1, 22–30). At the beginning of creation he was active in producing it. At its end he will be there to receive it as his own. Throughout all its course from beginning to end he keeps it together. "All things have been created through him and for him; he exists before all things and all things cohere in him as a system." Without him the universe would fall apart into chaos and nothingness. Even the scientists and the technologists owe their living to him!

Parallel thoughts are expressed in Hebrews 1:2–3. Christ is Heir of all things—everything has been created for him. Through him God made the worlds—everything has been created through him. He bears all things by the word of his power—everything coheres in him. He is the stamp, the impress, of God's real being—he is the image of God.

This is not philosophic speculation, interesting only to reflective thinkers or spinners of theories. It has a practical value for the Christian. Behind all the majesty of the universe, with all its beauties and all its terrors, is not just the great First Cause or the Unknown God. Behind all its mysteries is One whom we have seen as Jesus of Nazareth. If he is responsible, all must be well, even when storms rage and lightning strikes. And when men are disposed to be proud of their stupendous achievements, like landing on the moon—and they are stupendous—we can turn from the temptation to idolize men to bow before him who made it all possible. The scientists and the astronauts were but observing the laws of nature—and Christ Jesus invented them and keeps them operative.

If Christ is thus the Creator and Sustainer of all things, it is not surprising that "in him are hidden away all the treasures of wisdom and knowledge" (2:3). It must be so. In him all the fullness of deity has its permanent residence—bodily (2:9). There may be an allusion here to the incarnation. Though the Lord's body is now glorified it is still a body and he is still incarnate. He has taken manhood into the Godhead. The main point is that the complete deity in Christ is no mere shadow (2:17).

It is something to have a theory—or rather a Person—to explain the universe. But what is to happen to those who dwell in it? Christ is not only Creator: he is the Redeemer. Paul speaks of "the blood of his cross" and of presenting us holy and blameless, subject to no accusation, in the sight of God. The blessing is received by faith and we must not in fickleness move away from the hope of the gospel. We have been "qualified" to take up our position with God's people in the light. God rescued us from the authority of darkness and transferred us to the kingdom of his beloved Son. In him we have redemption—the forgiveness of sins (1:12–14, 19–23).

What more could any man want? There is ample room here for knowledge, wisdom and spiritual shrewdness. Reflect on Christ in all his fullness and walk worthily so as to please him in everything. Do not be tricked by groundless arguments and the smooth persuasions of a velvet tongue and a voice like brilliantine. Be on your guard against the man who would captivate you with the traditional deception of a philosophy which has nothing in it. You must not let anyone boss you by imposing on you rules of diet or a calendar of religious festivals. They are but shadows. Keep the solidity of your faith—to match the reality of Christ. You must not

accept your expulsion by those who lower themselves to worship angels and enter a new field of "visions." Airy visions
they are, as useless as the gasbags who see them. They have
lost their hold (1:9–10; 2:4–5, 8, 16–19).

The tone of the Epistle is set in the first eight verses. Notice
the words and phrases which mean so much: faith, hope and
charity; the word of truth and the saints who have received
it; the gospel, the grace of God; and evangelism, for the gospel "came to you." The letter ends with warm personal greetings and the naming of individuals.

The Epistles to the Thessalonians and the Pastorals

It is not usual to compare the Epistles to the Thessalonians
with the Pastoral Epistles (1 and 2 Timothy and Titus) but
it is interesting. The Thessalonian letters are "early," perhaps
the earliest of Paul's extant letters, with the possible exception of Galatians. But though early, they were not written
immediately after his conversion but about fifteen years
afterwards. The Pastorals come toward the end of his life.

Both groups reveal a warmhearted affection and concern
for the recipients. But 1 and 2 Thessalonians were written to
a church; the Pastorals were sent to individuals. The apostle
had had a short and sharp, and effective, ministry in the city
of Thessalonica (Acts 17:1–10) and after thoroughly "upsetting" everybody had left suddenly and secretly. Some of
the local converts had had a rough handling. The gospel had
been preached with power and had been received with much
affliction. In the same way, Timothy was to take his share of
hardship and Titus had to deal with a rough and tough
people.

The bonds between apostle and people, between the leader
and his lieutenants, were strong. Once away from Thessalonica, Paul longed to be back with his friends there. He
wanted to see them for their own sake and he wanted also to
exercise pastoral care on the spot. He was concerned for their
stability and wanted to scotch the lying rumors and slander
about himself which might do damage to their faith. He was
no mountebank and did not covet their money or their praise.

Although he had managed to compress much Christian teaching into the period of his short visit, there were gaps in their faith to be mended and some problems to be solved. Similarly Paul wanted his friends Timothy and Titus. He dwelt on his early association with Timothy and needed him in his last loneliness. Titus had been left in Crete to deal with the local situation but, like a commanding officer, was to be "relieved" and return to Paul. Both Timothy and Titus had to face and resist false teaching and to consider questions of the ministry. The place of ministers figures in some measure in the Thessalonian letters also.

Without doubt, Paul's teaching had been clear and compact, representative of the main doctrines of the faith. But the Thessalonians were not masters of proportion. They had placed too much emphasis on the Second Advent and then an apparent disaster struck them. Some of their members had died. It comes as a shock to us to realize that in a new church in the land of the heathen there is such a thing as the first Christian funeral. The Thessalonians had never before had such an experience and it alarmed them. They strenuously believed in the Second Coming of the Lord. Now some of his disciples had died. Would they miss his coming after all?

Paul has to set them right. They will not miss his coming. He will bring the dead with him! Thus those who survive until the coming will have no advantage over the Christian dead (1 Thess. 4:13–18).

Within a matter of weeks news came to the apostle of further trouble. The Thessalonians were so enthusiastic for the Second Advent that they had fallen into a panic by a tale that it had already occurred. It had happened and they all—not only the dead—had missed it! Some still looked to the future with conviction and stopped working. They sat down, as it were, to wait for it. Paul had to write at once to straighten them out. The Advent is imminent—but will be preceded by signs. Meanwhile they must work and not get the church a bad name by being parasites.

The "last days" are not absent from the Pastorals, though they are not there so prominent. Other matters have to be settled. The church has to be "organized"—though not over-organized. When converts have been made, they are not to be left high and dry, a mere company of people without guidance or help. They need pastoral care and teaching; not only must the convert be made but the church must be planted, or there will be no second generation growing up as a result of local nurture and evangelism.

It had been the apostle's practice to appoint presbyters or elders in every local company of believers. In the Pastorals, his long experience in this field is set down in certain standard requirements. If a man is to be made a bishop, a presbyter or a deacon, he must first pass certain tests. It has sometimes been thought that the necessary qualifications are very ordinary. On the contrary, they are marked by a shrewd and sanctified common sense. They might well be applied in any type of society. You may choose a bishop from a company of farm laborers, business executives, scholars or scientists, but it is still desirable that he has a sober home life, is able to teach others and can get along with them, and is above reproach.

The qualifications may be vital rather than pedestrian, but the subject is not perhaps inspiring to the reader. Two answers are possible. The passages had to be written and the directions given, and they are for the benefit of the church of God. But in the midst of such matters there are other treasures which certainly do inspire. There are great doctrinal affirmations in both Thessalonians and the Pastorals which remind us of the wealth of Christian truth. They are like the flag which a man long resident abroad suddenly sees fluttering before his eyes. It reminds him of home, of all the love and resource and security waiting for his return. The "great texts" may not tell all the story; not one of the Thessalonian or Pastoral Epistles is an Epistle to the Romans. But each text reminds us of the great truth by which we live. It suggests it, signalizes it, guarantees it. And in a situation which does not grip the imagination or turn a shuffling movement into a brisk step forward—like getting people back to work, cooling their excited eschatological miscalculations or framing rules for admission to the ministry—the great text has its relevance.

The Epistle to the Hebrews

Rather different in style and content is the Epistle to the
Hebrews. It dispenses with the usual salutation and plunges
straight into the subject, though the ending is more con-
ventional. "The friends from Italy" send their greetings, but
it is not clear whether they are actually in Italy or not. The
author asks his readers to bear with his "word of exhorta-
tion." It is certainly that. They seem to have been in danger
of slipping back either into Judaism or into heathenism. Before they do go back they ought to realize what they are
leaving. The letter is thus an essay with a mighty subject—
the finality of Christ. God has said, done and given everything in him and there is nothing to be added—not even a
postscript.

In the past God had spoken to the fathers in the prophets.
He had spoken in a fragmentary way, piece by piece and bit
by bit. There were thus many isolated pieces of revelation
but they had not been joined together. God had spoken in a
variety of ways, and men heard his Word as law and sermon
and psalm, and they "saw" it in signs and types. Now all the
scattered pieces are brought together and the utterance is
made to men in one mode, that of divine personality made
man (1:1-4). After all this rich though broken variety, he
has spoken to us in—a Son. In his Son, God has one voice
and one medium.

The writer first sets out the Son's relation to the universe
(cf. the section on Colossians). It is his: he created it and
he keeps it in being. The divine glory streams forth in him
and he bears the hallmark of deity. He is Master of his own
creation and creation cannot impede him in what he is to do.

For what God said in Christ is deed as well as word. God
spoke—and what he said was Christ; and never man spake
as this Man; and he hath done all things well. God's revelation of himself in his Son is summed up in two great acts.
First he made a purification from sins. This concentration on
the cross corresponds to Paul's "word of the cross" and his
determination to know nothing save Jesus Christ and him
crucified. Secondly he took his seat on the right hand of the

majesty on high. There is no longer any need to stand: his work has been done.

Before going on to describe in detail how the work was done, how the purification was made, the author pauses a while to survey the scene around him. In the thought of his day, the world was in the possession of the angels. They were masters of it and they "ran" it. This he cannot tolerate. In a series of scriptural proofs he shows that Christ is superior to the angels. He is no mere angel: he is the Son, to be worshiped by the angels. At best they are tenuous beings, as evanescent as the breeze or the flickering flame. His throne is forever, and a righteous throne as well. Earth and heaven sprang into being from his hands, but in time they will waste away like old clothes and be discarded and perish. But Christ abides, never to fail in years or character or power, in majestic session on God's right hand, waiting (all he has to do is to wait) until God makes his enemies his foolstool. The angels are but servants, sent in the interests of those who are to inherit salvation (1:4–14). The readers must not drift by neglecting so great salvation (2:1–4).

We do not now see everything subordinated to angels. To whom or to what is the world subordinated? If we follow the example of our author, we shall look at everything which is regarded as supreme and then affirm in triumph that it is subordinated to Christ. What is in possession? What does hold the field? Some would say science, some political power and dictatorship, and some even trade unions or organized crime and the underworld. None of them finally rule. All are under the final rule of Christ.

The readers must not stumble at the sufferings of Jesus, the humiliation of the cross. The Pioneer of our salvation had to taste death for every man, and this required him to participate in our flesh and blood. Only so could he be our High Priest, merciful, and faithful (2:5–18).

Bring your minds to bear on him. He is superior as a Son to Moses who was a faithful servant. Harden not your hearts! At this point the author gives a Bible reading from Psalm 95:7–11, emphasizing "Today." The way in is still open (Heb. 4:6–9). Hold on to your confession (4:14).

(This explains the use of the Venite—Psalm 95—early in the service of Morning Prayer in the Anglican communion. The uninstructed raise their eyebrows at the end of the psalm because it sounds so fearful. "Unto whom I sware in my wrath, that they should not enter into my rest. Glory be to the Father. . . ." It *sounds* dreadful; in actual fact it is not. They did not in fact enter Canaan. But in his mercy God has left the door open for us. The psalm is thus an invitation, appropriately placed at the beginning of worship.)

Jesus is our High Priest and of a distinctive kind. He has the rank of Melchizedek, not of Aaron (5:10; 7:1–28). He remains a priest forever and never goes out of office. His work on the cross is interpreted in the light of the Day of Atonement of Leviticus 16 (Heb. 6:19–20), where the tabernacle is a copy on earth of the heavenly tabernacle (8:1–6). In Jesus God instituted a new covenant because the first one did not work (8:7–13), the new covenant prophesied by Jeremiah (Jer. 31:31–34). The earthly tabernacle is described (Heb. 9:1–10) and attention drawn to its duality. There is an outer tabernacle or Holy Place into which the ordinary priests go constantly in the performance of their duties. Then there is a curtain, "the veil," and behind it the inner tabernacle or Holy of Holies. This is a restricted area and severely "off limits." Into it only the high priest can enter, and even he can go in only once a year and then only with blood shed and offered for himself and the people.

All this is richly symbolic. The Holy of Holies is where God dwells, and who can go in and meet him? Only one man and only once a year: the way in has not been opened up, at least not opened up in the Old Testament dispensation. It was a failure. The gifts and sacrifices were offered but they could not perfect the worshiper in his conscience. The cleansing was but ceremonial. He could not enter in within the veil and have fellowship with God.

But now Christ has come on the scene, the High Priest of blessings ready to be bestowed. This alters everything. The Levitical high priest ministered in the earthly sanctuary, the copy of the divine one. Christ did his work in the heavenly sanctuary, though paradoxically he did it while on earth at

its beginning. It is the work of the high priest on the Day of
Atonement—with significant differences (9:11–28).

Christ does not begin with a sacrifice for himself, for he
knew no sin (7:26–28). He did not use the blood of goats and
calves but his own blood to take him into the Holy of Holies.
He did not sacrifice a physically unblemished animal but
offered himself in the perfection of his own obedience. He
did not sacrifice an unreflecting animal, but he offered himself and knew what he was doing—carrying out an eternal
purpose. He did not put the sins of Israel on to the head of
a scapegoat, but he bore the sins of men himself. He did not
do it year after year but once and once for all. He did not do
it ineffectively, merely for the cleansing of the ceremonially
defiled, but effectively for the purifying of the inward man to
qualify him for fellowship with God. He did not enter into an
earthly Holy of Holies, a "copy" of the heavenly one, but into
heaven itself, now to appear before the very presence of God
for us. He did not go away like the scapegoat, never to be
seen again, but will be seen again at the End of history to
round off his salvation. Until then he is able to save those
who come to God through him because he is always alive,
always in office as a Priest and always interceding with God
for them. His salvation never fails (7:24–25).

Christ has achieved what was impossible under the first
covenant. The high priest entered the Holy of Holies alone.
He never took anybody with him, nobody followed him in
and nobody ever dared to try to enter. Now a new and living
way has been opened up through the veil into the very
presence of God. The veil is now no longer a barrier between
the outer and the inner tabernacle. The writer would have
relished the statement of what happened at the death of
Jesus. "The veil of the Temple was split in two from the top
to the bottom" (Mark 15:38). The barrier is down. Exclusive-
ness no longer reigns. All may come to God through Jesus,
the new and living way, through the crucified Jesus who is
the new veil through which we may pass. Let us all—not
only the old high priest!—draw near (10:19–25).

Maintain the confession; stir up love and good works; fail
not to meet together: the Day is drawing near. You know

about the one sacrifice: there is no other. To go away in sin can lead only to judgment. You have endured before: do not throw away your boldness. The Coming One will not delay. We are not the people to shrink back into perdition. We are people of faith, to gain, not lose, our soul.

There follows the famous eleventh chapter which lists the heroes of faith, the picture gallery of the New Testament. On the strength of it the author asks the readers to keep with him in running the Christian race, keeping their eyes on Jesus. He endured. Take that into account and do not weary and crumple up. You are not dead yet! Having a hard time? God is giving you the training of sons, sons whom he loves. Stiffen your sagging limbs and keep right on. It is fatal to fall behind the grace of God. And remember where you really are.

Well, where are they? It has been said that according to this Epistle we go to heaven every time we pray. The writer puts it more picturesquely. You have come to Zion. You have come: you are therefore already there. You are at Zion, mountain and city of the living God, the heavenly Jerusalem with its myriads of angels and the church composed of those who have received privileges, the first-born registered in heaven. You need not wait for the holy city of Jerusalem to come down out of heaven (cf. Rev. 21:10). You are already there. The holy city will come down from God, but you have already come to him, to God the Judge of all.

To God the Judge? Whom even the ancient high priest could approach only once a year, and he alone? Yes, for you have come to Jesus, Mediator of the new covenant, and to his sprinkled blood which speaks more eloquently than that of Abel. Abel's blood cries from the ground (Gen. 4:10): "Vengeance! Keep him out." Jesus' blood speaks softly to the ready Father: "Mercy: bring them in." There they will find others at the Father's side, the spirits of just men made perfect.

Do not turn away from this. It is Zion, not Sinai; grace, not law; heaven, not earth. To trifle is more dangerous than at Sinai. Thank and worship God through our Lord Jesus, whose kingdom will never be shaken, and live the Christian

life, with God your Helper. Do not lose your bearings in the
squalls of doctrines. Make for home: Jesus Christ, the same
yesterday, today and for ever.

The Epistle of James

The Epistle to the Hebrews is perhaps the most "Jewish"
of the epistles in the New Testament. If it is, the Epistle of
James runs it a close second. For James is a Christian Amos,
with a marked emphasis on Christian duty. This is important.
It is sometimes said that men steeped in the Old Testament
and its sacrificial system would be bound to think of our
Lord's death as an atonement, to dwell on his blood and to
be absorbed in his cross. The Epistles to the Romans and to
the Hebrews are thus historically conditioned and are no
more than we might have expected. Of course we now know
better. . . .

This makes the atonement itself historically conditioned,
but we can now dispense with it. It is a specious argument.
For James was as much steeped in the Old Testament as
Paul or the author of Hebrews. If the argument is sound, he
ought to have spent all his time—and his space—on the
sacrificial cross. In fact he did not; he does not even mention
the blood of Christ. He is concerned with behavior. If the
cross of Jesus is no more than an example which influences
believers, how is it that James can challenge believers for
having faith but not works? Faith without works is dead: so
much for the merely moral influence of the cross.

James cannot stand the waverer, the double-minded man,
the "man of two minds" (1:6–8). But he is no mere moralist,
an ethical teacher with no gospel. He is deeply concerned
with morals, but it is behavior inspired by the Christian faith
and not apart from it. He has been accused of attacking
Paul's doctrine of justification by faith, but this is to mis-
interpret him. Paul's question is, how can the sinner get out
of the dock? His answer is, believe on the Lord Jesus Christ.
Thus by the exercise of his first faith he does get out of the
dock. If James meets such a man some time later, he asks
him some searching questions. "So you began to believe in

Jesus, did you? Sinner though you were, you were accepted by God when you put your faith in Christ. Is that correct? Well, what have you been doing since then? Has your faith made you a better man? What kind of conduct has it inspired? If you are still leading the same old life, your faith has not made any difference to you, has it? That cannot be justifying faith!" Paul would agree (Rom. 6:1–2; 1 Cor. 7:19; Gal. 5:6).

The faith, the gospel received, must be applied. That is the point James is concerned to make. The Christian life is not an armchair but a workshop. If a man has really received the gospel in faith, he will work. For James, insistent on good conduct as he is, has a gospel.

James sees that "mercy triumphs over judgment" (2:13). He speaks of himself as the *slave* of the *Lord* Jesus Christ (1:1; cf. 2:1), thus implying that he has been redeemed. He tells his readers to "receive the implanted Word which is able to save your souls" (1:21). He is by no means always critical of faith but can speak sympathetically of faith in our Lord Jesus Christ (2:1). He recognizes the preaching of the gospel and its acceptance, the work of God in the heart and regeneration (1:18). "Of his own will he gave us birth by the Word of truth, so that we might be a kind of first fruits of his creatures." He recognizes conversion, saving souls, forgiveness (5:15, 19–20), knows about those elected to be "heirs of the kingdom which he promised to those who love him" (2:5), and gives a side glance to what looks like baptism (2:7). He anticipates the Second Advent, the Parousia of the Lord which is near (5:8).

James has a sound gospel foundation on which to build an insistent demand for the performance of Christian duty.

The First Epistle of Peter

The First Epistle of Peter resembles the Epistle of James in seeking to exhort rather than to expound. But Peter is not so much up in arms against abuses as protective. He seeks to inspire the people of God scattered about Asia Minor to live the Christian life as well as to profess it and to equip them to face any outbreak of persecution. So far the attacks on Christians do not seem to have been the outcome of a universal law against Christianity as such. Persecution was not yet organized policy formulated by an anti-Christian state. It arose here and there, now and then, sometimes from ill-affected neighbors and sometimes from the excessive enthusiasm of officialdom. There seems to have been no "pattern" in the attacks to suggest that they were "master-minded." The fact that they just "happened" tended to keep the Christians on their toes and perhaps to fray the nerves of some. They had no civil security. Peter seeks to steel them for the uncertainties of life on earth.

What may be called his method is instructive. The term *method* is not the best. It speaks of calculation, of thinking out the best line of approach, whereas Peter wrote from spiritual instinct rather than from reasoned principles.

The salutation in the first two verses reminds the readers of who and what they are. It sets the standard, lays the foundation, creates the atmosphere. Remembering that some of the recipients were slaves, numerous enough to warrant a section of the Epistle to themselves, at the beck and call of their owners for any and every task, with no rights of their own except to be used as tools and to be treated at times with harshness and plain unfairness because of their masters' bad temper, we can but observe that the author sets his sights very high. Slaves they might be, but what possessions they have!

In common with the other believers, they are the elect of God. Except when attention is drawn to them in outbursts of persecution, they are lost in the general crowd. Simple, humble, unrecognized though they are among men, they were singled out and chosen by God in eternity. This is "strong meat" appearing in the first course. They were chosen in the sphere of the Spirit's sanctification. They were chosen to be made holy by the Holy Spirit, not to be trained as, say, mathematicians or carpenters by human teachers. They were chosen to obey God's call by responding in faith and in consequence to be sprinkled with the blood of Jesus. Thus they were qualified to draw near to God and to be in fellowship with him who had made them his choice. Banned by humans, they are welcome in God's home.

Peter has finished his opening greeting, but he finds that he has opened the floodgates. He cannot stop. Sheer praise to God streams forth from him as he remembers and writes down what God in Christ in his faithfulness has done, is doing and will do. Even angels desire to stoop down to see more clearly the sufferings destined for Christ and the consequent grace destined for men (1:3–12).

Then Peter draws his inference: "Therefore" (1:13). He wants his readers to "gird up the loins" of their mind, mentally to pull up their long flowing robes and tie them round their waist, ready to run, stripped for action. Brace your minds; be on the alert. They must pay attention and be keen to obey the call of duty: the life of holiness and of Christian conduct; and of cheerful and innocent readiness to face attack if it comes. We should not miss, as we read the Epistle, that persuasions to duty are based not on mere commandments but on Christ's redeeming work—from which they have gained everything they have and are.

There is always the challenge to love God and man, each in his separate situation: duty to the state, to slaveowner, to husband or wife. Sometimes there will be need to suffer. Be ready. Remember your Redeemer. The Epistle ends with a terse "Peace to you who are in Christ—all of you." It will not fail to come.

The First Epistle of John

The First Epistle of John is likewise addressed to "you," but it lacks a formal salutation and the mention of names and places. It seems to be addressed to a situation and has been thought to be something in the nature of an encyclical letter—a message for Christians over a wide area.

It is sometimes imagined that John was a dear old man, kindly, benevolent, but without depth, whose only concern was to repeat "little children, love one another." That is very far from the truth. John may have been old, but he had an acute mind and his Epistle is highly articulated: he does not

just go wandering on. He brings before his readers a series
of tests. For example, note the repeated "if we say" (1:6, 8,
10, KJV) and "he who says" (2:4, 6).

He writes to people who do not require information. "I am
not writing to you because you do not know the truth but
because you do know it" (2:21). Then why does he write? It
is because there were people trying to lead them astray
(2:26). Their impact had been far from devastating (4:4),
but he urges his readers to keep the original message which
they had heard and to abide in the Son and in the Father
(2:24, 27).

Never forget: the Christ is Jesus (2:22) and Jesus Christ
has come in the flesh (4:2). It is antichrist that denies and
antichrist is already in the world in great numbers (2:18;
4:3). They—in the pew or in the pulpit—are deadly enemies.
They stand for opposition in the guise of similarity. They
look like preachers and teachers but their purpose is to
undermine the faith. They are still with us. To repudiate the
Son cuts off fellowship with the Father. To confess the Son
is to have fellowship with the Father also (2:23). Note the
unity of Father and Son.

John's opening paragraph is stark in its material reality.
Jesus Christ has indeed come in the flesh: we have heard him
and seen him. We gave him a long look, stared at him and to
prove that he was real we touched him, felt him, handled
him and gripped him. He was no fleeting spirit but flesh and
blood as we are.

John is so sure of his facts that he sees everything in black
and white, as "either . . . or." As weak mortals we ourselves
may not always know whether a man is a believer or not. We
have to balance knowing a tree by its fruits with a refusal to
judge. Every pastor feels the weight of this. Is a rebuke in
order? But God knows and John is giving God's point of view.
He accordingly makes some basic distinctions.

If we regard the church as composed of true believers, the
church is one thing and the world another. "We" are of God
and we are the church. The world hates us, it is not to be
loved but conquered, and it is passing away. The unit of the
church, the man who does the will of God, abides forever
(2:15; 3:13; 5:4). We abide in the Son and in the Father

(2:24; 3:24; 4:13). The world lies "in the evil one" (5:19). It is in his power. It is "occupied territory."

The distinction between life and death is absolute. "We have passed from death to life" (3:14). There is no midway position which is neither one nor the other, no "no man's land," no high seas belonging to neither side. We either have eternal life or we do not. "He who has the Son has life; he who has not the Son of God has not the life" (5:11–12).

Similarly, truth and falsehood are incompatible. "No falsehood is of the truth" (2:21). The implication is that a false doctrine or the denial of a true one cannot be slipped in unobtrusively and regarded as part of the content of the Christian faith. In John's Second Epistle the recipients are not to receive a man bearing false doctrine and are not to bid him godspeed. That would be to participate in what he does (2 John 9–11).

There is a clear distinction between the children of God and the children of the devil (1 John 3:10). There is no vagueness in John's mind here. A man may be "not far" from the kingdom of God, but however near he may be, he is not yet inside and not yet a child of God. There is a corresponding cleavage between doing righteousness (not talking about it) and committing sin. The former is of God and the latter of the devil (2:29; 3:7–8, 10).

Finally John has a distinction to account for what we might call an inattentive congregation. "He who knows God listens to us; he who is not of God does not listen to us" (4:4–6). This is a test for both minister and people, and is still relevant.

Other Epistles

At this stage we now merely point to the existence of a few small Epistles, not unimportant but not greatly adding to Christian doctrine. It is doubtful if any basic doctrine could be founded on them in isolation. The Epistles are: Philemon, 2 Peter, 2 and 3 John and Jude. Philemon is a winning note to commend a runaway slave, now converted, to his Christian owner. 2 Peter in one passage takes us back to the majesty of the Transfiguration.

6.

The Revelation:
The Whole Church Eternally Exulting in the Gospel

THE BOOK OF THE REVELATION is what it claims to be, an apocalypse, an "unveiling." What had hitherto been unseen is within view. Without divine aid man could never pierce the obscurity, but God has made the gift. The hidden future is unfolded. Distant heaven is brought near to us. Indeed, John takes us with him into heaven and back again. He has been given visions and he shares them with us who read.

The book is also prophecy. The author is a prophet, not a mere visionary. He sees what God wishes him to see and he writes it down. Blessed is the man who reads it out loud to an assembled congregation, and blessed are they who hear and keep what is written in the prophecy. When we share the vision we receive not only "information." There is an element of command, which we must keep. John does not give us entertainment but inspiration and challenge (1:1–3).

The revelation and the prophecy are in the form of an epistle, a letter. The three introductory verses constitute a sort of heading with a subtitle. John is giving us the Word of God and it is linked with Jesus Christ. The Word is always weighty but especially now: "the time is near." After such an introduction John greets the seven churches in Asia with the customary "grace to you and peace from. . . ." From whom? John's description of God is noteworthy: "He who is and who was and . . ."—we expect "and who will be" but John does not say this. He says, "who is to come" or "the Coming One." God not only "will be" for all eternity in the transcendent realm, "in heaven," as we say in the Lord's Prayer. He will come and make his impact. For, as John has said, "the time is near." The theme of the book is apparent.

Grace and peace come also from the Holy Spirit in his fullness, represented by the seven spirits before God's Throne, and from Jesus Christ. John cannot refrain from speaking in his praise. He is the Ruler of the kings of the earth. He loves us still and he loosed us from our sins which bound us with their guilt and power, not with a knife or any instrument but with his own blood. The Ruler of kings is the Christ of the cross. He gave us a royal status and made us priests, men with the right of access to God. And he is coming with the clouds, to be seen by all, even by those who had pierced him. God is to come. Christ is to come.

From this awe-inspiring thought John turns to tell us something of himself. Because of his preaching of the Word of God and his witness to Jesus he had been exiled to a small island. "I was in Patmos," a rugged, unpromising island, and "I was in the Spirit." On the Lord's Day he heard behind him a loud sound as of a trumpet speaking. What he saw he was to write in a book and send to the seven churches. He turned "to see the voice" and he saw "a Son of Man like." (Some people still talk like this.) What he saw can hardly be visualized by us. John is given *ideas* about the majestic Jesus in the form of fragmentary *pictures*. He is to write down the things "which you saw and which are and which will come to pass after this." This seems to correspond with him "who was and is and will come," though the order is different. As instructed, John obediently writes down the letters to the seven churches. Each has its distinctive message and yet all the messages are for all the churches—and all the church. He who has an ear, let him hear what the Spirit says to the churches. (1:4–3:22)

Then John saw in heaven a door wide open and heard the same voice bidding him "come up here." He would see "what must take place after this." John is prepared for a divine inevitability. At once "in the Spirit" he was struck by the awe-ful picture of the divine sovereignty and authority. He saw the throne of God, and God seated on it, surrounded by unceasing worship. From the throne proceed flashes of lightning, rolling peals and claps of thunder. In front of the throne is a sea of glass, a motionless sea. No wave troubles it, no heaving swell to suggest the breathing of the bosom of the deep. It is flat and still, like a sheet of ice.

The meaning is plain. Lightning strikes and thunder completes the terror and warns of future flashes. The sea is a separating sea. Keep out! It is an ancient veto given in another idiom: not the cherubim with whirling and gleaming sword (Gen. 3:24) but the inanimate elements of fiery lightning and the cold sea.

For the vision thus far shows no trace of a Messiah. It is God the Creator who is worshiped, the eternal All-Controller who willed creation into being.

Consciously or unconsciously John is preparing us for visions yet to come, partly by his use of images and partly by his concept of God. The "four beasts," better, the "four living creatures," were full of eyes, symbols of the divine omniscience. The imagery, both here and elsewhere, is alien to us, but we may guess that the language of apocalyptic was as understandable in John's day as references to "Uncle Sam" or "the Russian bear" are to us. Just as God is omniscient, so he is omnipotent. He has everything in his own control and he does what he wills. Nature is plastic in his hands, to be bent and shaped and used precisely according to his purpose. History is part of his purpose and he brings it to its foreordained end. But that is the problem.

Throughout history a bitter conflict has been going on. God has his purpose indeed and men do not readily fall in with his commands. But behind men and women is a malignant power ever at work to destroy all that is good, to counteract all that God plans and does and to bring ruin on the human race. It is more than a power, more than a "life force"—or rather, more than a death force. It is intelligent, capable, personal, thinking, and operating not as some great statesmen who "think in continents" but in the vast world itself and through all the length of time. It is beyond the wit and ingenuity of men to master. The moral and scientific cream of humanity are helpless before his cunning and his stratagems. Moral and political schemes and philosophies remain but mere theories. The thinkers and the common man cannot put theory into practice and implement the victory.

Who will win? God's sovereignty is working for victories in history but what will be the outcome of history? History itself gives no sure answer. But there is an answer. John found it when he passed from the Creator (4:1-11) to the Redeemer (5:1-14).

Not that he left the Creator behind! For it is still the same vision, still the same place and he still sees the One seated on the throne. But there is an additional Figure now, not perhaps absent before but certainly unseen by John. God is holding a sealed book in his hand and an angel is loudly proclaiming the need for someone to come forward and open it. Nobody in the whole universe can open it or see its contents. John is in tears. It is the book of history and destiny. But nobody knows the final result of the conflict, the outcome of history.

An elder reassures him. There is Someone who is worthy to open the book. He is the Lion of the tribe of Judah, the Root of David. John looked and saw—not a lion but a Lamb still bearing the marks of having been slain. It is clearly a vision of Jesus Christ. It is he and he alone who holds the key to history. All others fail—great military conquerors, political rulers, profound moralists, scientists of every kind.

We should not fail to notice that John does not see the world's supreme theorizer. Christ can open the book in virtue of the conquest of his cross. And he does not merely understand the contents of the book. He has implemented them. What he has done by and in virtue of his cross has solved the problem. There is now no question of the outcome of the conflict between the divine purpose and the evil opposition, between God and the devil. Christ has conquered. And more: he is in the midst of the throne. He is no person brought in from the outside, as it were, apart from God. At the very center of the sign of God's utter sovereignty, the throne, is the Lamb, still bearing the scars of his passion. At once he is acclaimed in worship, for he was slain and has redeemed by his blood. The new song is louder and ever louder as myriads join in universal adoration.

> The whole creation join in one
> To bless the sacred Name
> Of Him that sits upon the throne,
> And to adore the Lamb.
> —ISAAC WATTS, "Come let us join our cheerful songs"

The Father planned it; the Son accomplished it; history is the scene of it: and the outcome is assured and certain. Victory!

It is a victory gained once for all in principle. Its benefits are reaped by installments. Its final flowering is yet to come. For we are concerned with the whole Christ, living, dying, rising—and coming. In his ministry he cast out the devil's underlings by the Spirit of God and by the finger of God (Matt. 12:28; Luke 11:20), thus demonstrating that the kingdom, the royal rule, of God had already come. He bound the hostile strong man and began at once to plunder his property (Mark 3:27) by making disciples. Men entered—the kingdom of God. After his death, the decisive battle of it all, and his resurrection and exaltation, his church made known the deeds of the Redeemer. Disciples were made; converts kept coming in; the plundering of the enemy continued. With every new convert the kingdom "came."

Thus the church wins lesser victories. For she is the church militant and she inevitably endures sufferings. This is the reason for the question about the final outcome. Who will finally win? The church knows the answer because the Redeemer is the Christ who not only came but will come—in his Second Advent. John knows that the tempo of the conflict is rising and he writes to encourage and inspire the embattled members of the church militant. The time is near. The Lord is coming. Final victory is in sight.

Shortly before that glorious End there will be a number of messianic judgments in history. John describes them symbolically in three series, the seals (6:1–8:5), the trumpets (8:6–11:19) and the bowls (15:1–16:21). The series appear successively in the book, seven seals, then seven trumpets and finally seven bowls. But as they happen in history, just before the End, they are really one event, described from different points of view.

In these three blocks John has not kept all the time to his immediate subject but has made some insertions. Thus between the sixth and the seventh seals (7:1–17) he intersperses the sealing of the servants of God and a moving picture of their exultant worship at God's victory and of his tender presence with them. Between the sixth and the seventh trumpets (10:1–11:13) come "the little scroll" and the "two witnesses." History is approaching its End ("no more delay"), and under God's protecting hand the church must both witness and suffer. John then speaks of the utter rivalry between church and evil, evil embodied in the civil state, the empire.

The seventh bowl, the last of the messianic judgments, is elaborated (17:1–19:10). The last bowl of the wrath of God is drunk and drained by the imperial city, "Babylon." The great city falls and great is the fall thereof, to the lamentation of kings and merchants and seafarers, whose economic seduction by her has led them to share her spiritual ruin, and to the exultation and praise of heaven.

Then comes the Second Advent of Christ (beginning 19:11). He advances in glorious majesty. Evil is subdued. Christ's kingdom is manifested in history, judgment is administered and executed for the last and final time and the new creation appears. John is promised a sight of the bride, the wife of the Lamb, and he is shown—a city! It is the holy city of Jerusalem, coming down out of heaven from God. It symbolizes the people of God, among whom God eternally dwells—for their eternal security and blessedness: no night, no danger, no sin. His servants see his face and worship him. The throne of God and the Lamb is in the midst of his people. For this glorious End—the beginning of eternal joy—"come, Lord Jesus." And while we wait, "the grace of the Lord Jesus —with all."

We must now go back and give some thought to a surprising feature. When Christ comes, the devil is seized and

chained, enclosed and sealed: put away where he can do
no harm for a thousand years. Then he is released—after
Christ's reign for a thousand years—to attempt the havoc of
conquest. It is in vain. He is flung into the lake of fire and
sulphur forever. Does the renewed outbreak imply the weakness after all of Christ or a sporting second chance for the
devil?

It does not. The principle of God's creation, the Eternal
Word, and the Ruler of the kings of the earth does not find
the devil too strong for him even for a limited period; and
infinite goodness would not give a sporting chance to the
embodiment of all evil. How then are we to view the millennium?

First, it should be noticed that the kingdom of God comes
in history. It has so come before, in the historic Christ. It
came in the days of his flesh and is embodied in him. It
"came" with every new convert who received the gospel
from the preaching church. At the Second Advent it will come
in its final realization, when the prayer, "Thy kingdom come,"
is finally answered. And it will finally come in history. For a
thousand years—if this figure is to be taken literally—the
kingdom of God will be here on earth.

This is not a "rehearsal" or an experimental period. The
kingdom will have really come. But this earth with all its
wonders and glories and this universe with its vast reaches
of space are yet too cramping a situation. Eternity is a long
time and the earthly environment would stale before the
inner riches of the kingdom. It therefore passes to the transcendent realm.

The millennium reveals also that in another way the environment is not enough. We have seen that no human agency
can solve the problem of sin or ensure the victory of good
against evil. Bring on your thinkers and their agents; pass
your laws and devise your schemes; with all compassion
relieve the poor, educate the ignorant and heal the sick; give
all state aid to every kindly welfare agency: and what happens? Some will want more than their share and some will
despise and even dislike their fellows. Sin cannot be dis-
lodged by an environment.

They have tried it in Britain. In 1945 a socialist government came to power—not simply to office. They set out in all sincerity and earnestness to create a classless society. Ten or twenty years later they were confessing with sorrow that they had failed. In the old days a feudal lord looked down on his serf. Today in suburbia they try to keep up with the Joneses, and the distinctions between Jones and his neighbor are minute. But they are there. The proletariat, though few will confess to belonging to it, have their representatives who preach the class war. The kingdom of God is not eating and drinking but righteousness, peace and joy in the Holy Ghost. Sin arises from the human heart and even the perfect environment of the millennium does not prevent it. In the human heart the devil has something on which to work.

The devil will be "released." He has his own diabolic schemes and purposes, but they are all within the control of God. Evil has its reserves, illustrated on a small scale by the sinful man who keeps coming back to his counselor with new arguments against the Christian faith and his own surrender to Christ, but the reserves are never too strong for the living God. God uses the devil for his own loving purposes, just as he once used Cyrus (Isa. 45:1). He makes him, if not his servant, at least his tool. At the end of the millennium evil is brought out into the open, smashed and swept out of the universe forever.

We are reminded of the garden of Eden. There too was a perfect environment and there man fell. But at the end of the millennium with its perfect environment there are more than man and wife. Before the eyes of multitudes right is vindicated and evil condemned and abolished. And thus we shall be forever with the Lord.

There are two further points for brief comment. We read of the wrath of God and of the Lamb ("their wrath" 6:15–17), and that the Lamb (not a butcher!) will be their Shepherd and God will wipe away every tear (7:17). Implied is the unity of Father and Son and the unity of justice and mercy. The Father is one with the Son in the grace of the cross and the Son is one with the Father in the upholding of righteousness. Both grace and wrath express the one divine character.

The second point is concerned with the quaint and delightful statement that there was silence in heaven for about half an hour. This arresting remark (8:1) is more than a biblical oddity. The worship of heaven itself is hushed in a breathless silence in order that the prayers of God's people may be heard. The answer is positively hurled to the earth with resounding effect (8:5). It is the will of almighty God that the judgment of sin and the coming of his kingdom is not simply an exhibition before spectators. It is an answer to his people's prayers.

A postscript of a general nature must now be added. John saw in vision the fall of the city, the end of Rome and its empire. In actual fact the empire continued and went on in time officially to adopt the Christian faith. What has gone wrong? Has John made a ghastly mistake?

Nothing has gone wrong and he made no mistake. As an obedient disciple he lived in expectation of the End. It might come as a thief in the night. When he looked out on to the final struggle and the final victory, he saw the conflict between the forces of good and those of evil embodied in the final manifestation of organized society. He saw in vision the last secular society; he saw, surrounding him, the Roman Empire. We have to disentangle the two. In his vision of the End the Roman Empire would get in the way!

We might attempt to put it like this. A lecture is to be given, with slides shown from a projector. The school auditorium is prepared: the projector is put in place and the screen, a fixture, is unrolled. Then it is found that the device to control the focus is stuck. Nothing can repair it and the image on the screen is all out of focus and quite useless. Then somebody starts to experiment. Could they rig up an alternative screen, somewhere between the original, fixed screen and the projector itself, where the picture shown would be in focus? It was thought to be a good idea and the search was begun for something to serve as a screen. It was a large old tapestry portraying ancient Rome, with some of its buildings erect and some in ruins. It was decided to use it and the pictures shown from the projector came out well—apart from the fact that ancient Rome blended with the scene. Even so the lecturer was able to give his lecture and it was agreed that he had indeed "illustrated" it well. Rome did get in the way but the pictures were not spoiled—the audience was merely slightly inconvenienced.

It is something like this with John. He looked forward (from his "projector") to the End (the fixed screen), but the immediate context of his life (the tapestry of Rome) modified what he saw without serious distortion. His message is thus still relevant for the militant church here on earth, fighting her spiritual battle and—if she is faithful—still watching.

7.

The Certainty of the Gospel

THE BOOKS OF THE BIBLE have often been given "popular" titles which sum up their contents or call attention to some outstanding feature. For example, the Book of Genesis has been called the book of beginnings, Job the book of suffering and the Psalms the book of song and of experience. In this spirit we might well express the impact which the New Testament has made on us by describing it as the book of certainty.

Certainty can be a dangerous term, if the philosopher was correct in saying that "the psychological feeling of certainty does not in itself give the assurance of epistemological validity." This is a learned way of saying that a man who is dead certain may prove to be dead wrong—and perhaps in consequence just dead. We always have the crank with us: the man who is certain that his lost cause is right and still worth a fight; the man who is certain of his remedy for everything, whether it be a policy or a pill; even the lunatic who is certain that he is a fried egg and is ever looking for a large enough piece of buttered toast to lie upon, or that he is Napoleon and must find the Duke of Wellington to settle accounts.

There is another danger. Some people wish to "prove" the Christian faith and thereby ensure that they can really be certain. Such a certainty would be the death of the Christian religion. For it would put God out of our lives; or, perhaps more correctly, it would never admit him. Consider what such a proof would involve. We should have to start with the evidence. This would have to be formulated in propositions which constitute the premises of an argument. From the premises an inference is drawn, a "conclusion." If the premises are true and the reasoning is logical, the conclusion is likewise true. The conclusion itself may be used as a premise to be combined with another premise, and from the two a further conclusion may be drawn. Thus we might have a chain of argument. But the final result would be no more than a conclusion. It would be a true conclusion but it would be only a conclusion, a proposition, a statement which could be written down.

We might be able to state with complete truth and satisfaction that God exists and might describe his character and acts with considerable detail. But it would be still something just said or written down. We should not encounter the living God. We might indeed address prayers to him in our certainty of his existence and character, but we should have no faith. It would be quite unnecessary. Why have faith when you already know?

God has not chosen this method. Those who trust him most fully know him most deeply. "By faith we understand." It is no good if a man with a scientific education or the taste of a philosopher quarrels with this. He cannot dictate to God and it would be a pity if he chose to go to his own place for the sake of an obstinate whim.

Now our purpose is not to "prove" the Christian faith. We rather hope to look at some features of certainty as they appear in the New Testament. If enough of us looked long enough and entered deeply enough into the same experience, we might under God transform the present Church Hesitant into a church which goes out conquering and to conquer. We should no longer be content to listen to the world, to discuss, to pat the "other religions" on the back for the good fellows which they are. We should "go, tell," come wind, come weather.

We notice first the language of certainty used in the New Testament. It strikes us in the words of its vocabulary and in the tenses of the verbs. Let us begin with the vocabulary.

In his Preface (Luke 1:1-4) Luke tells his reader what he has done, in order that he may have full knowledge of the certainty of the subjects of his instruction. This is no airy "sure, I'm right." The price for certainty has been paid in purpose, labor, effort, pursuit, patience, and no doubt at times in disappointments and frustrations.

Abraham was *convinced* that God was able to do what he had promised (Rom. 4:20-21). "He staggered not" (KJV) in regard to God's promise, though nature itself seemed to be against it. The Thessalonians received the gospel when the apostle preached it to them with ringing conviction, and they entered into his certainty. At any rate they unconsciously copied the evangelistic party in the combination of suffering and spiritual joy when they received the Word and they went on to be evangelists themselves. What made them? They had already endured much affliction. Why add to it? It can only be because of their inner certainty, for which they were prepared to pay the price (1 Thess. 1:5-10). Paul had already paid it in the outrageous treatment he had received at Philippi (1 Thess. 2:2).

The writer to the Hebrews asked his readers to join him in drawing near to God through Christ with the certainty of faith (Heb. 10:19-22). It was not mere theory. They had already known joy and suffering for their faith (10:32-34). In his famous eleventh chapter he illustrates time and time again what is done and suffered by men of faith, and the faith is not "watery." These were men of conviction and they not only paid for their convictions: they were ready to pay. Their anchor was "certain" (Heb. 6:19).

We have already encountered "boldness" (p. 57). It is part of the vocabulary of certainty. It is ultimately based on knowledge. Eternal life is to know the only true God and Jesus Christ whom he sent (John 17:3). Such knowledge Paul already possessed. He regarded it as of surpassing worth and the object of unceasing pursuit. But how could he seek what he already had? Just as a man may start a journey, or begin to sing, or fall ill time and time again, so Paul was intent on renewing his initial acquaintance. He longed to "get to know" his Lord, Christ Jesus (Phil. 3:8–10). His knowledge was partial (1 Cor. 13:9, 12), hence his perpetual quest. But the world did not know God at all (1 Cor. 1:21). The heathen do not know him (1 Thess. 4:5), and there are those who refuse to know him and will be punished for it (2 Thess. 1:8). The apostle was prepared to pay for the certainty of his knowledge, for he sought "the fellowship of his sufferings." At the end he could say that "I know him," and suffer for it without shame (2 Tim. 1:12). Men given to religion might seek the "unknown God" (Acts 17:23). Paul knew him in his Son and proclaimed the One whom he knew.

Paul knew the Person. He had made his acquaintance and he kept it. He also knew the facts about the Person. "We know that Christ, raised from the dead, no longer dies; death no longer lords it over him" (Rom. 6:9). He knew the facts about divine providence. With those who love God, who have responded to his call and are thus in line with his purpose, "we know that all things work together for good" (Rom. 8:28, KJV). He has seen it happen. They "work together" because God in his loving sovereignty makes them work together. He has seen it. And he has experienced it. He has known afflictions but they do not damp his exultation. "We know that affliction produces endurance, and endurance in its turn produces the tried experience of the veteran. ('It's only gunfire. Don't worry. We've heard it all before.') This yields hope; and our hope never embarrasses us with its failure" (Rom. 5:3–5). He has seen it; experienced it; and tested it. He has been through it all, with all its possibilities of questioning and despair, and after every kind of test he can say that "I am persuaded." He looks back over a history of hardship. Like young ladies who after formal education are sent to a "finishing school" to fit them for polite society, so Paul through the years has received the finishing touch of manifold adversity. He is convinced, sure and certain (because he has stood the test) that neither the obscurity of death nor the agonies of life; neither the hostilities of men nor the malignancies of demonic forces; neither nature nor supernature; neither the bitter present nor the unknown future; nothing, nothing at all in the whole wide world will ever get the power to separate us from the love of God in Christ Jesus our Lord (Rom. 8:35–39).

Ancient texts have a habit of startling us with an entirely new application. Think of two Christians today who walk where Paul walked. One is the pilot of an airplane, the other a submarine commander. Could we blame them for a false interpretation of Scripture if in danger they steeled their endeavors by remembering the tests and triumphs of the apostle? "Height will not separate" cries the airman. "Depth will not separate" answers the sailor. Both set off on their mission with this conviction. Both find it true in the crisis.

We pass now from the terms of the vocabulary to the tenses of the verbs. In some contexts and with some meanings they are highly suggestive. The simple past tense (aorist as it is called) highlights our *rescue.* "God saved us" (2 Tim. 1:9). This fulfills the purpose of "the Lord Jesus Christ, who gave himself for our sins in order that he might rescue us . . ." (Gal. 1:4). The spirit of the deed is illustrated by the life of John Wesley. When he was only five years old his father's old rectory at Epworth caught fire. The family had escaped the blaze when suddenly the face of the little boy was seen peering through one of the windows. A villager ran to it, another climbed on to his shoulders and they reached the child just before the roof fell in. Wesley never forgot the awful moment and it became for him the sign of his later evangelical conversion. In two senses he was "a brand plucked out of the fire." Such is the rescue of those whom "God saved."

Another past tense is the perfect. It does not merely record the deed but brings it up to the present moment in its effect. Thus "you have been saved" (Eph. 2:5, 8) means that "you are now safe." It implies *reflection* and *relief,* reflection on the past act and relief at the present position. "Christ has been crucified" (cf. 1 Cor. 1:23; Rev. 5:6) does not mean that he is now on the cross or that he is dead but rather something like "he remembers his cross; he still bears the scars; his work is effectively done." The "it is finished" of John 19:30 means "it has been brought to its end," "the work is now complete" and therefore "the blessing is available."

With the present tense we see a *possession*. "He who has the Son has life . . . I am writing this to you in order that you may know that you have eternal life . . ." (1 John 5:12–13). Believing men possess God's gift here and now.

When the future tense is used, a *prospect* opens before us. "Having been justified . . . having been reconciled, we shall be saved" (Rom. 5:9–10). Looking toward the future does not imply human uncertainty on the lines of "I thought I was saved; I now find that I shall have to wait for salvation. Shall I gain it?" It assures us of the faithfulness of God, faithfulness toward his Son's work for us and in us. Salvation, already received, will be enjoyed in all its fullness. Peter combines both prospect and possession. The inheritance is reserved in heaven and you meanwhile are being guarded, for a "salvation ready to be revealed at the last time . . . you are overjoyed . . . obtaining the goal of faith, the salvation of souls" (1 Pet. 1:5, 8–9).

Rescue, reflection and relief, possession, prospect: it should be observed that these great themes are not derived from the tenses as such, but from the tenses of certain verbs. It is this fact which gives us such an impressive demonstration of Christian certainty.

Why is language used in this way? It is because of a second feature, the foundation of certainty.

The foundation of Christian certainty is fact—not idea, aspiration or hope. The Christian faith contains ideas and it would not be the Christian faith if it did not. But it is not simply ideas, however good. Christians aspire and hope and it would be a sad day if we ever gave up aspiring for deeper worship, stronger commitment, more devoted witness, more sacrificial work. It might be even worse if we gave up hope. The idea, the aspiration, the hope: each is of importance but no one is *the* important element. Central and foundational to the Christian faith is the fact of Christ.

This is made crystal clear by what was said when the early church went out from the temple into the streets, from the gathered group to mingle with men. The public speakers stated—and proclaimed—facts. "Jesus of Nazareth, a man demonstrated by God to you . . . you slew, whom God raised up . . ." (Acts 2:22-24). "The God of our fathers glorified his servant Jesus, whom you delivered up and repudiated before Pilate when he had decided to release him. You repudiated the holy and righteous One and asked to be favored with a murderer. You killed the Pioneer of life, whom God raised from the dead, of which we are witnesses" (Acts 3:13-15). "The God of our fathers raised Jesus, whom you dispatched by hanging on a tree. Him God exalted to his right hand as Pioneer and Savior, to give repentance and the forgiveness of sins to Israel. We are witnesses who attest all this, and so is the Holy Spirit whom God gave to those who obey him" (Acts 5:30-32).

Here are a few samples of the "proclamation" scattered through the New Testament. It was preaching the "Word." Peter is so certain, that he can tell us that the Word of the Lord abides forever and that "this is the Word which was preached to you as gospel" (1 Pet. 1:24-25). The sermon may not last forever but its content will—and be evidence at the Day of Judgment.

The facts are plain and can be simply summarized. God did it; he now offers it ("we are witnesses"); we ourselves received it (or else we too are still in our sins, 1 Cor. 15:17). But what is "it"? It is Christ in his truth: who he is and what he did and what God did in him. Men do not enter dangers and risk their lives for nothing. The hostility which surrounded the early preachers and which did not deter them is the measure of their own certainty. The facts which they proclaimed were true.

Certainty has its language and its foundation. We must now examine what we call the confirmation of certainty. We see it in the lives of individuals and in the wider circle of groups, of the fellowship, of the church. Take the individuals first.

The apostle Paul once said that he himself, the Pauline ego, was no longer living but that Christ was living in him. In one sense he had to be living or he could not have made the statement. He therefore explains. The human life which now in fact he does live "I live in faith in the Son of God who loved me and delivered himself up for me" (Gal. 2:20). As a rule men do not like to be in debt, especially if they are constantly being faced with demands for repayment. Paul gloried in a debt he could never repay. He was infinitely and forever in debt to Christ for his love, brought to its focus in the cross. There, of set purpose, knowing what he was doing and by his own deliberate choice and will, not avoiding what he could have avoided, for very love the Lord gave himself up to death—"for me." Paul gloried in the cross (Gal. 6:14). He was absorbed in it, absorbed in the Christ who lived in him. This is not a form of pantheism or a dulling of his own sensibilities or an obliteration or even a cramping of his own personality. It did not put his personality into low gear. It quickened it, sharpened it, intensified it, made it.

A diplomatic man, whatever he privately thought and felt, would have exercised caution and restraint. Christ and his cross were a stumbling block and foolishness (1 Cor. 1:18, 23; Gal. 5:11). Why ask for trouble? Why preach a message in such terms as will upset the listeners? Why expose yourself to accusations of foolishness? Why "put their backs up"? It was partly because Paul had been commissioned to do just this and partly because he gloried in it; but it was not least because called, authorized and sent as he was, he was absorbed in this same Christ who lived in him. In short he was possessed of certainty before which opposition, accusation and adversity meant nothing to him. Nothing could undermine it—toil and drudgery, the lash and imprisonment, stoning and shipwreck, danger and betrayal, cold, hunger and sleeplessness, with the added burden all the time of care for the people of God with all their stupidity and waywardness and division and sin. He had the dominant purpose of a certainty which nothing could dislodge (2 Cor. 11:23–28).

Paul was no crank, a man with one idea and obsessed with it. He had the witness of the Spirit (Rom. 8:16), the poise and confidence of the accepted son. The Spirit gave him both knowledge and language, enlightened Paul and through him enlightened his listeners. The Spirit played his beam upon

the face of Christ and loosened the apostle's tongue (1 Cor.
2:9–16). He brought him through the horrors which would
have finished other men, by helping him in weakness (cf.
Rom. 8:26). He helped him, not by relieving him of his load
but by shouldering some part of it himself, thus giving his
servant the inspiration of companionship.

In all the many changes which beset him, Paul was able
to adapt, to reorient himself, not with the changeableness
of the chameleon but with the versatility of the master of
the situation (Phil. 4:11–13). Whatever the "weather," the
fruit of the Spirit could grow in him (Gal. 5:22–23). Like a
friend of his on one occasion, he could risk his life for the
sake of Christ's work (Phil. 2:30). If we called it a gamble,
we should have to add that it was a "sure thing"—a "cert"!—
because of the hope which lived within him. Christ had put
death out of action (2 Tim. 1:10), and through Christ had
come a comfort and encouragement which was eternal (2
Thess. 2:16). Certain of his facts and of his own experience,
Paul could draw an inference. God's gracious act in Christ
has led to our justification; then let us enjoy peace with
God. This logical inference (Rom. 5:1) is followed by a
"practical" inference. You see all God's grace in Christ and
how you have responded to it and received it; therefore
present your bodies as a living sacrifice . . . (Rom. 12:1).
The certainty of the reasoning process matches the certainty
of a man in Christ.

The confirmation of certainty is thus seen in the life of an
individual. But it is not individualistic or isolated. The apostle
is not the one exception. For example, the Holy Spirit is
received by *an* individual and witnesses with "our (individual) spirit," not merely our spirits collectively (Rom. 8:16),
as a body. We each have only one spirit or are only one spirit,
but we all have the separate experience. Hence Paul can
naturally speak of the plural "children of God." In a parallel
passage he says that God sent the Spirit of his Son into our
(plural) hearts (Gal. 4:6). A fellowship is implied, a fellowship of men and women of like experience. We each and all
have the Spirit and in principle (unless, e.g., weak in faith,
Rom. 14:1) have the certainty and the certainties already de-

scribed. On the Day of Pentecost the Spirit was given to the fellowship, to "each one" and to all (Acts 2:1–4). This gift has never been withdrawn from the church. On the contrary God continually gives his Spirit, who is a river rather than a well (cf. the section on Philippians).

Two consequences follow. From the Day of Pentecost onward through the centuries the church in the power of the Spirit has been able to make converts. If this were not so, the church would have died out. In theory the church is always in this danger. Every generation will be followed by the next. Will the next believe? In every generation which has followed the Day of Pentecost there have been converts to Christ and the church as a company, a fellowship, has continued. And when the converts have been made it has been through the Holy Spirit that they have grown in holiness.

The making of converts confirms the certainty. It is through the ministry of the Holy Spirit that the cross is not emptied of its power (1 Cor. 1:17).

The second consequence is of perhaps more immediate relevance. Through the permanent presence of the Holy Spirit in the church, its constituent members, believers, are able to communicate with one another. They must preach to the world, but in a sense they cannot communicate with it—there are too many "natural" men (1 Cor. 2:14). Until the Holy Spirit lays hold of them they remain outside the circle of those who "understand." Believers can and do speak to one another and they "understand the language." One man speaks of his own debt to Christ and others know exactly what he means. They are in debt also. He tells of answered prayer, of comfort in sorrow, of a troubled and a relieved conscience; he says that "the Lord has laid something on his heart" or that he hears God's voice calling him onward. They understand. They have walked, and they still walk, that same road. All who are in Christ have a hidden life, "hidden with Christ in God" (Col. 3:3). They are all on the same side of the dividing line, the line which separates them from the "natural" man. They enjoy the same scenery and speak the same language.

Now in the fellowship of the redeemed, the certainty of the most convinced is increased even more. There are no doubt individuals of such sure faith and certainty that they are willing to go to the stake if need be. There certainly have been such. But in the Christian community a man of conviction looks around and finds others like him. They too believe; they too are convinced; they too have their certainties; they too can and do say, "I know him." The authentic church is the fellowship of the convinced, of those who are sure, of those who know.

If anybody looks at the Church Hesitant and is skeptical of the foregoing paragraph, it is an answer to say that not all who are of Israel, are Israel (Rom. 9:6); not every person who looks like a Jew is a Jew but only the one who is a Jew in the secret room of his heart (Rom. 2:28–29; cf. Matt. 6:6). So not every person who "looks like" a Christian is a believer; not everyone who nominally believes really believes. "Your circumcision has become uncircumcision" (Rom. 2:25). Your baptism has become unbaptism. In making this distinction we are not thinking of a select few but of an innumerable company of sincere believers dispersed throughout the world, united to one another because united to Christ, sure and certain of that by which they live: they have tested and proved it in the hurts and tears and perilous fascinations of life.

In this little study of Christian certainty in the New Testament, one factor stands out clearly. A typical believer—"a certain man"—stands in a certain position. His outlook may be summed up thus:

> Upon a life I did not live,
> Upon a death I did not die—
> Another's life, Another's death—
> I stake my whole eternity.

The certainty may appear to outsiders as no more than a "psychological feeling." But the stake is high. The believer is glad to take the risk, unafraid because he has the peace of God and with deep joy because he returns the love which Jesus Christ has given to him.

Finally we must dwell on the certainty of certainty. Early in his Christian life the New Testament believer is baptized. Almost all shades of denominational thinking now recognize as an academic truth the fact that in the New Testament it is converts who are baptized. This is a test of their "feelings."

Baptism involved publicity, commitment and possibly danger. It was not just a prayer for all sorts and conditions of men, in which the candidate might be included—with plenty of anonymity. He stood in the public eye. How many unbelievers would be prepared to undergo a public washing?

Here the inner faith and aspiration are, as it were, seen. No longer can a baptized man or woman evade the claims of Christ; no longer can they say that what they thought was faith was just a vague aspiration. They have come out into the open and publicly committed themselves to Christ. Witnesses could remember the event. Today it might even be discreetly photographed. Of their own free will and choice they have taken the oath of allegiance. To go back on it would be to become a renegade. They are publicly committed.

And it might put them in danger. Their conversion might have been associated with a riot, with a frenzied mob and outraged officials. They were mixed up with those who speak of "another King"—Jesus. The uproar might die down but would persecution break out?

Their first formal profession of faith, their public initiation into the church which outwardly told the story of their personal and private initiation into Christ when they first believed, was thus charged with certainty from the beginning. In those early days and amid those early conditions, men were sure.

As practicing believers and living in Christian fellowship they continued in the apostles' doctrine, in particular in the breaking of bread—the Lord's Supper or Communion Service. Here, again openly because in the company of others, they renewed their allegiance to Christ and "took the sacramental oath" to him. They did it openly and they did it regularly, first testing themselves and then eating and drinking, remembering the Lord's death and its meaning for them, both as gift and claim. They not only read or hear. They see bread broken and wine poured out and with their mind's eye they see again the broken Body and the shed Blood—for them. Conscience is challenged, resolve strengthened; the heart is opened both to renewed self-dedication and to the renewal of the Holy Spirit and a still stronger grasp on Christ.

Why the repetition? Why the regularity? Why the possible inconvenience and the probable blows of conscience? Why go on with it all? Why indeed, unless the believer retains the certainty with which he began? This is precisely what he did: he kept his certainty, but it was a certainty which grew and matured as he himself grew and matured in Christian faith and life.

Life itself is always uncertain. We never know what a day may bring forth and "in the midst of life we are in death." But as we advance in years the uncertainties inevitably increase, especially the uncertainties of health and life. But with the believing man the inner certainty grows rather than diminishes, and as he draws ever near to his "end" he looks forward to the day when he "will see him face to face." And of that he has a sure and certain hope.

We have tasted the fine fare of the New Testament and savored its many flavors, grave and gay, present and future: justice and mercy, the church and the world, Christ and his people. But it is only a taste. We must not be content with the taste. We must go on from the sip to the full draught, from the preliminary dainties to the whole course, from the course to the meal itself, and finally to the very Messianic banquet. In the meantime, God has yet more grace and truth for us to savor, as it breaks forth from his Word.